Understanding
the
Haftarot

An Everyperson's Guide

Rabbi Charles Simon

A Project of the
Federation of Jewish Men's Clubs

outskirtspress
DENVER, COLORADO

Understanding the Haftarot: An Everyperson's Guide
All Rights Reserved.
Copyright © 2012 Federation of Jewish Men's Clubs, Inc.
V1.0

Any quotations or translations used were excerpted from the Jewish Publication Society Bible Commentary.

Outskirts Press, Inc.
http://www.outskirtspress.com

The FJMC (Community, Innovation, Leadership) empowers its members, Jewish men and their families, to become more passionately engaged in Conservative/Masorti Jewish life. Its programmatic initiatives transform individuals and synagogues into more vibrant communities across the globe.
Website: www.fjmc.org
Facebook: FJMC_HQ
Twitter: @FJMC_HQ
LinkedIn: http://www.linkedin.com/company/fjmc

Paperback ISBN: 978-1-4327-9743-0

PRINTED IN THE UNITED STATES OF AMERICA

DEDICATION

This book is dedicated to my longtime teacher and friend Neil Gillman, who challenged me to make it better, and to Max Kadushin z'l and the many muses in my life.

ACKNOWLEDGMENTS

This book would never have seen fruition if it weren't for the encouragement and support of the following:

Michael & Jo-Ann Rapaport
Richard (Dick) Goldfinger
Benjamin Zucker, in honor of Charles Zucker
Randy & Anita Borkenstein
Michael Freilich & Barbara Freilich
Ira Barfield
Donald & Barbara Grenadir
Marlene & Larry Ritter
Greg & Linda Gore
J.B. & Lynette Mazer
Ernest Smolen in memory of Hazzan Alan Smolen —
    "The tree does not stand far from where the apple falls"

The Leadership of the FJMC Seaboard Region

B'nai Torah Men's Club, Boca Raton, Florida
Beth Shalom Men's Club, Livingston, New Jersey
Etz Chaim Men's Club, Marietta, Georgia

And my dear supportive Colleagues:
Harold Berman
Shalom Lewis
Mel Sirner
Micah Hyman
Elliot Dorff

ENDORSEMENTS

"Rabbi Simon has illuminated the portion of the Shabbat service that has acquired a mere quasi-ceremonial status because it is typically assigned to the Bar/Bat Mitzvah of the week, and has transformed it into a genuine learning experience. He has provided us with a rich tapestry of historical, theological and inspirational sources which place each haftarah in its own unique setting and enabled us to understanding how it fills its unique role in the worship service. A significant contribution to the educational work of the synagogue."

Rabbi Neil Gillman is the Aaron Rabinowitz and Simon
H. Rifkind Emeritus Professor of Jewish Philosophy
at the Jewish Theological Seminary

"In *Understanding the Haftarot* Chuck Simon has made the Prophets come alive. With his knowledge of Biblical history and keen sense of drama, Simon gives context and familiarity to the men and scenes of the Haftarot. I recommend this book to all who are seeking deeper understanding and clarity of sequence in the weekly prophetic readings."

Cantor Nancy Abramson,
Director, H. L. Miller Cantorial School
Jewish Theological Seminary

"If the Haftarot are to reclaim their rightful place as a primary pedagogic tool for uncovering and imagining the Torah's deep truths for the modern synagogue attendee, then Rabbi Simon's exquisite, erudite and thorough introduction to the material offers an essential backdrop to each of us, clergy and layperson alike."

Aaron Alexander, Dean
Ziegler School of Rabbinic Studies
American Jewish University

"Rabbi Simon has provided a valuable contribution toward garnering spiritual meaning from our comprehensive

Shabbat liturgy. Rather than viewing the Haftarah cycle as a random array of sacred texts, he has constructed a useful and inspiring framework. Combining historical context with thematic assessments, this volume brings the weekly Haftarah to life. Side-by-side with the Torah portion, these prophetic readings are intended both to elevate the soul and to strengthen our ties to Jewish Peoplehood, past and future."

Rabbi Alan Silverstein
Current Chair of the Foundation for Masorti Judaism,
Past President of both the Rabbinical Assembly and of the
World Council of Conservative/Masorti Synagogues

CONTENTS

Preface
Why I Wrote This Book

I began to seriously and methodically study haftarot in 2008, where it became my custom to deliver a mini-*d'rash* (explanation) about the weekly haftarah in a minyan that I attended in Great Barrington, MA. At the same time, having written these *derashot*, I would share them with the leadership of the Federation of Jewish Men's Clubs (FJMC). The haftarah explanations developed a following and in 2009, Stan Greenspan, one of the officers of the FJMC, sent an email, without my consent, to the FJMC Board of Directors, announcing that I would write a weekly haftarah commentary and anyone who registered could receive it. By the time I read the announcement and called him to express my anger and to chastise him for what was clearly an inappropriate act, more than one hundred people had already registered. The following week, *The Unraveller*, a weekly haftarah commentary, made its first appearance. Three months later more than fifteen hundred people were receiving it weekly.

Two year later, I was sitting in schul on the first day of Sukkot preparing to read the haftarah, which was excerpted from the book of Zechariah. I flipped the pages forward and noticed that the haftarah chanted on the Intermediate Shabbat of Sukkot was excerpted from the book of Ezekiel. "Isn't this strange?" I thought. "Zechariah lived approximately fifty years after Ezekiel concluded prophesying. Ezekiel's contemporary was Jeremiah. Wouldn't it have made sense for the haftarah to be excerpted from Jeremiah?"

And then it hit me. It was possible that Ezekiel and Jeremiah knew one another or at least knew of one another! And it was possible, actually probable, that they knew of Gedaliah, the last ruler of Israel.

At that moment, on some level, my understanding of the Prophets changed. They were transformed from literary figures to actual people. People who had families and who lived and struggled just like we do every day of our lives. At that moment, on some basic level, I became a more connected Jew.

This was when and why I began to write.

Charles Simon

INTRODUCTION

I recently learned that certain right-wing religious groups recite the blessings before and after the haftarah and then read the haftarah silently. I have been in synagogues where the person or people chanting the haftarah chanted it in English. I have witnessed a number of people dividing the haftarah and have actually taken part in readings where one person chanted the haftarah in English while someone else chanted the haftarah quietly and dramatically in Hebrew.

I have spoken to colleagues who shorten the haftarot in their synagogues and others who hope to eliminate the haftarot from their Shabbat morning services in order to save time. Haftarot are under siege.

This is surprising and a bit confusing because one can actually learn something about Judaism from studying the haftarot, while one can rarely learn anything from repeating the same prayers week after week. The liturgy, for the most part, is repetitious. The haftarot are always different.

I remember when I was in rabbinical school, my Talmud teacher explained that Jews traditionally learned Bible by studying Talmud. Judaism, he told us, differed from Christianity in a number of ways, one of which was the way one learned Bible. He explained that Christians learned Bible by studying it book by book, while Jews, with the exception of the study of the Torah (the five books of Moses, which are often studied parasha by parasha), learned about the second and third divisions of the Bible (i.e., the Prophets and the Writings) by studying Talmud.

The rabbis who organized the Talmud used quotes from the books of the Torah, the Prophets and the Writings, as proof texts to help them resolve legal situations. For example, a quotation from Leviticus, Isaiah, or Psalms would be considered a valid proof text in a discussion of law. The system was hierarchical and based on their understanding of revelation.

Quotes from the Torah superceded quotes from the Prophets, which took precedence over the books in the third section of the Bible, the Writings. When in the midst of a Talmudic discussion a text was quoted, the student would need to find it, and in doing so would learn a little about the biblical text being referenced. It might be, for example, that while discussing the laws about wine, a rabbi would quote a verse from the story of Samson, who was prohibited from drinking wine. As a result the student might end up reading and learning the story of Samson. This method of learning Bible didn't teach Jewish history because the students of the time understood the Samson story theologically. This was and continues to be a faith-based system of learning for those who choose not to live in the contemporary world.

This system worked for them, and to a great extent still works in the fundamentalist world, but it doesn't necessarily work for us.

The haftarot have always challenged me. For the most part I could never fathom why they were read, and most of the time I found the language to be confusing. Yet they have endured, or rather we have endured them, for nearly two thousand years.

If the haftarot can't be accepted as faith messages, how can they be accepted and what can they teach us? Perhaps they were intended to be inspirational? It's possible, but it seems to me that even if one reads them in English they are nearly impossible to comprehend, let alone to understand how they should inspire us.

Perhaps they were intended to help us become more aware of their corresponding Torah portions? After all, the texts that were selected as haftarot spoke to generations that might have needed a more contemporary connection to make the Torah portions meaningful. Unfortunately, the ways the haftarot were organized sometimes make it difficult for us to understand their messages and why they were connected to a particular Torah portion. One would think that if we understood the connections to the text, our understanding of Jewish life would be enriched. Unfortunately, in many instances, the connections are too tenuous to be credible or were presented in a way that no longer resonates.

I have met people who find some haftarot beautiful or memorable. Usually that's because they connect to a poetic phrase that resonates with meaning; for example, "He shall reconcile parents with children and children with parents" (Malachi 3:24) or "What does God require of you? Only to do justice and to love goodness, and to walk humbly with your God" (Micah 6:8).

These are beautiful phrases, but the people for whom these phrases resonate do not necessarily accept the haftarah as an inspirational document. Resonant phrases do not explain why a particular haftarah is connected to a specific Torah portion, nor do they provide the necessary background for understanding the Prophet's message. Frankly, memorable phrases or faith- based acceptance leaves me cold.

If one studies the development of our liturgy, one can learn about the development of Judaism in a limited way, but the study and teaching of haftarot provides a greater awareness of the forces that shaped our present. This awareness can enrich Jewish identity and help us connect and understand how we have been shaped historically. It is even possible that it can impact upon the nature of the choices we make.

In order for haftarot to be meaningful, it is necessary to read them through two lenses. The first lens is to understand the time in which the haftarot were allegedly written. In addition to learning Jewish history, this provides the context to understand why a specific text was chosen. The second lens challenges the reader to view the text from the point of view of the rabbis who selected them to serve as haftarot.

The haftarot, as we know them today, are a result of a process which most likely began in Maccabean times, 2nd century B.C.E., and came to a conclusion some five to six hundred years later. The rabbis, through a process of which we can only surmise, made these selections because the passages they chose reflected their hopes, fears, and desires.

What are the haftarot?

The haftarot are excerpts from the second part of the Bible known as "The Prophets." The Prophets are broken down into three categories. The first six books are referred to as "the Former Prophets." This is followed by the "Major Prophets" (Isaiah, Jeremiah, and Ezekiel), and finally, the "Minor Prophets," called "the twelve." This covers a time period that begins with Joshua around 1200 B.C.E. and ends just before 445 B.C.E.with the last prophet, Malachi.

In 460 B.C.E. Malachi, accompanying a priest named Ezra, journeyed from Babylon to Jerusalem. Ezra travelled with a retinue of more than eighteen hundred people and with the authority of the Babylonian Empire. He carried with him a scroll. The rabbis assumed that this scroll was the Torah. They credited him for instituting its reading on market days, Mondays and Thursdays, and establishing the minimum number of verses which can be read once the Torah has been opened. The rabbis also accord him the honor of decreeing that the Torah should be read during the Shabbat afternoon (mincha) service. Whether Ezra was responsible for the implementation of the reading of the Torah is uncertain. It is also questionable if he actually brought the entire Torah with him.

We do know from the eighth chapter of the book of Nehemiah that it is recorded that "Ezra the Scribe, having recently arrived from Babylonia, assembled the people on the first day of the seventh month (Rosh Hashanah) and presented a book of the Law of Moses to the congregation in a solemn service. Ezra blessed the Great Lord God, as the people shouted amens, and in turn rose and prostrated themselves." If one carefully reads Nehemia 8:14–15, it is possible to infer that on the second day he recited a passage from Leviticus 23:25–27 which refers to Sukkot.

With the establishment of Torah readings, prophecy as an institution in Israel ceased. From this point onward, inspiration would no longer occur through visions or the hearing of voices, but only through the study of the written word.

A three-year Torah reading cycle was established in Israel, or at least in Galilee, according to Professor Ben Zion Wacholder, who wrote about this in 1970. It is referred to as the triennial cycle, while an annual Torah reading cycle was established in Babylon and also possibly in parts of Israel at the same time. A great deal of uncertainty exists about the origin of these cycles and exactly how the triennial cycle actually functioned.

It is unclear why and how two different calendar cycles were established, whether or not they occurred simultaneously, or if one predated the other, because the first reference to a selection from the prophets being read occurs in early Christian times.

Six to eight hundred years later, while our ancestors were living under Roman occupation, the calendar shifted from a triennial reading to an annual one, possibly as a result of the more dominant Babylonian culture. Go figure, the Babylonians and the Romans used an annual calendar. According to our tradition, the person responsible for this shift was a man referred to as Rab.

The haftarot can be grouped into what I understand to be a series of nexus points—that is to say, they appear to be organized around specific ideas or events.

The first nexus point is comprised of a series of haftarot which were excerpted from the books of Joshua, Judges, and the first book of Samuel. These haftarot focus on the need for a central government in order to defend the Israelites from the many tribes which were attempting to take back the land they had lost.

The second nexus point consists of excerpts taken from the 2nd book of Samuel and the first book of Kings. These haftarot are concerned with the nature of kingship and the establishment of the Davidic line. They highlight the rise and fall of the reigns of Saul, David, and Solomon.

One generation after the death of Solomon, Israel split into two kingdoms, often referred to as Judah and Israel, or the northern and southern kingdoms. This is the period of

Isaiah, Hosea, Amos, and the Minor Prophets. Many of the haftarot selected around this nexus point preach to the Northern Kingdom, "Repent! Return! God will take you back, it's not too late."

But it was too late, because in 722 B.C.E. the Northern Kingdom was conquered by the Assyrians, and from that point onward they were referred to as the "ten lost tribes."

Imagine if you were one of the rabbinic leaders living after the destruction of the 2nd Temple and you read these texts. You learned that if you strayed from the ways of our ancestors and worshipped other gods, you would vanish from the face of the earth just like your northern ancestors! The words of the prophets leading up to the devastation of the Northern Kingdom must have been understood by the rabbis as a fearful warning. This is the focus of the third nexus point.

The fourth nexus point begins one hundred years later during one of the few times that Israel existed as an independent kingdom. It focuses on King Josiah and the discovery or the writing of what we believe to be the book of Deuteronomy. After reading the book of the Law (Deuteronomy), Josiah began to enact a series of laws that transformed Israelite society.

He replaced the current form of local government by the elders with a priesthood. He abolished local sacrifice and mandated that all worship (sacrifice) would take place in Jerusalem. Finally, he connected two distinct festivals, one of unleavened bread and one commemorating the liberation from Egypt, into one festival which today we call Passover.

The haftarot in this nexus, like their predecessors, have theological implications—i.e., if one follows God's ways they are rewarded with prosperity, and if they turn away from the Lord's ways it will result in poverty, humility, and exile. The haftarot that complete this nexus lead up to the first and second exile and the ultimate destruction of the Temple which took place in 586 B.C.E.

Did I say first and second exile? Yes, because in 597 B.C.E., as a result of a series of poor political decisions, Nebuchadnezzar, the king of Babylon, uprooted and exiled a significant portion of the upper classes of Israelite society. One of these exiles was the prophet Ezekiel. Thirteen years later, and as a result of some less than wise political decisions, Jerusalem was destroyed and the second exile occurred. This was the time of Jeremiah and Ezekiel.

Very little is known about what occurred in Israel from the time of the second exile (586 B.C.E.–460 B.C.E.) until Ezra; however, a great deal is known about what life was like in Babylon during this period. Our ancestors were uprooted and settled in a suburb of Babylon. As a people we can surmise they had only two ways to respond. They could either assimilate or become more insular. They did both.

Living in a separate part of the city, they became more insular. Shabbat observance became part of the community's culture. This was before the existence of prayer books and before the mitzvot of Shabbat observance, and all other mitzvot as we know them, were established. It is possible that they didn't work on Shabbat and perhaps prepared their meals in advance, but I doubt they were concerned with when they should recite the Shema, or what would happen when someone stirred a pot of beef stew with a dairy spoon, or tore toilet paper or violated any other of the mitzvot that are recorded in the Talmud and reflect discussions that occurred centuries later.

Our ancestors also assimilated into the larger, more sophisticated Babylonian culture. Over time, our ancestors assumed Babylonian names, like Mordecai, Esther, or Zerubabel, who was one of the last rulers of Israel. Zerubabel means the "seed of Babylon." The names of our months were also changed from what they were called in Israel. Rather than referring to the months as they were referred to in the Bible, "first month," "second month," "seventh month," the names were changed to Babylonian ones—Adar, Nisan, Heshvan, Kislev, and so on.

The final nexus point focuses on the desire to rebuild the Temple and what happened once this occurred. In 539 B.C.E.

Cyrus, the then emperor of Babylon issued a decree permitting the rebuilding of the Temple. Our ancestors believed Cyrus to be an instrument of God and a sign that God was working to return his people.

This was the period of our final three prophets, Haggai, Zechariah, and Malachi, and what we refer to as the time that second and third Isaiah lived. Haggai and Zechariah were contemporaries and took part in the Temple's rebuilding. Malachi, who lived some fifty years after the Temple had been rebuilt, assumed a traditional prophetic role and was critical of the manner that the priests were behaving.

Six to eight hundred years later, our ancestors living under Roman occupation studied our holy texts and understood them to be warnings. The incidents leading up to the disappearance of the Northern Kingdom and the destruction of the Temple served as a poignant reminder to those who recalled the circumstances leading up to the destruction of the Second Temple. The words and messages of the prophets reached across hundreds of years and offered comfort and guidance to our ancestors, who were concerned with the preservation of Jewish life and Judaism as a way of living.

When the switch from a triennial cycle to an annual one occurred, the size of the haftarot was also expanded. The combination of the annual Torah reading and a more developed prophetic reading made the Shabbat worship service significantly longer.

Why did they do it? Wasn't a full Torah reading, especially when accompanied by all the other liturgical prayers like Hallel and Musaph, enough? What motivated them to further lengthen the service?

I suspect that the transition to an annual cycle reflected a strong emphasis to foster the study of Torah. Our ancestors proclaimed, "*Talmud Torah keneged koolam* (the study of Torah outweighs everything)," or as Rabbi Akiba said, "Study is the highest form of worship because study leads to practice."

Our ancestors believed that our people's survival depended upon our people learning to study our holy texts. This was their solution to keeping them from straying like their/our ancestors did before them. The haftarot were intended to be tools to increase the knowledge level of the people. The rabbis made certain that all prophetic readings ended on positive or hopeful notes because they desired positive engagement.

Do you remember what the Yom Kippur liturgy says? "Prayer, Repentance, Tzedakah overturn the severe decree." What was the severe decree? It was the burden that people felt after the Second Temple's destruction. They believed they were responsible both individually and collectively for the behaviors of their predecessors. They were being punished for their ancestors' misdeeds.

It was Rabbi Johanan ben Zacchai, the first person to be called "rabbi," who taught that individual behavior could avert the severe decree. He abrogated the guilt of our ancestors and transformed Jewish life from what was viewed as a burden to one that embraced the ability of people to make a difference. The rabbis living a few hundred years later, the ones who selected the prophetic passages to serve as haftarot, were a product of that change. They were extremely careful to accentuate the positive and not the negative.

This book attempts to suggest a context to understand and possibly find meaning and value in the passages selected to serve as haftarot by the rabbis, our spiritual ancestors, some two thousand years ago.

How to Use This Material

This material has been designed to help the reader gain a general picture of the history of the prophetic period and to assist them to better understand specific haftarot.

Some people might use this pamphlet like a dictionary or an encyclopedia. Others will read it the same way they would read a regular book. Because of its dual nature, it was necessary to repeat a certain amount of the material in order to assure the reader obtains the necessary historical background.

The maps were specifically designed to provide a general picture of the times in question with easily understandable information designed to make this period more understandable.

I made a conscious choice to omit footnotes primarily because I was concerned that the inclusion of footnotes could discourage potential readers. While I believe my research is sound, I chose not to write an academic work. The tone of the book was meant to be inclusive and enjoyable, and I felt that the presence of footnotes would serve as a deterrent to potential readers.

It has always been my belief that knowledge of the past, specifically of one's people's past, impacts on the way one thinks, comes to view oneself, and can impact on how one makes decisions. This was most likely the case for the rabbis, who actually must have wrestled with one another when they were deciding which selections from the prophets should be considered haftarot. I think they selected these haftarot with a goal and in the hopes that understanding and relating to the messages of the prophets could shape the future of the Jewish people. The lessons they intuited from the texts of the prophets challenged them to actively try to shape our people's future.

It is my hope that one's Jewish identity and commitment to study will be enhanced as a result of developing an understanding of the haftarot. I also believe that this understanding is more than an academic exercise and can strengthen one's spiritual core. It might be that the rabbis living in the aftermath of the Bar Kokbah rebellion understood spiritual development and spiritual incite differently than many of us do today, but it shouldn't abrogate the messages or the value of the words of the prophets. They like we lived in tumultuous times and needed to navigate between the political and social reality of the times and their innate sense of dignity and ideal behaviors. Perhaps they expressed themselves as we need to express ourselves. Perhaps they wrestled with how to act in accordance with God's will in the same way that we do today. And finally, perhaps the rabbis who selected and inserted their messages into our services two thousand years ago did so with the hope that an educated person makes educated decisions.

TABLE OF PROPHETS

If you wish to read the background to the haftarah in question go to the indicated pages

Let's not forget Elijah and Elisha, even though they don't have their own book, a series of haftarot reflect their activities. See pages 14, 22, and 32–34.

Understanding
the
Haftarot

An Everyperson's Guide

TIME LINE

Nexus 1
Joshua–Judges

Nexus 2
The establishment of the Davidic line
1047–1007 B.C.E.   King Saul
1037–970 B.C.E.   King David
1001–931 B.C.E.   King Solomon
930–910 B.C.E.   King Jeroboam (son of Solomon)

Nexus 3
Two kingdoms divided
930–722 B.C.E.   Israel (Samaria) and Judah; Kingdom of
Israel falls to Assyrian Empire

Nexus 4
Destruction of the First Temple
715–687 B.C.E.   King Hezekiah of Judah
621 B.C.E.   Josiah
597 B.C.E.   First exile
586 B.C.E.   Fall of Jerusalem & second exile

Nexus 5
Cyrus and Can we ever really go home?
539 B.C.E.   Cyrus becomes Emperor of Babylonia
460 B.C.E.   Malachi and Ezra come to Jerusalem

NEXUS 1
JOSHUA–JUDGES

∙∙

Joshua, the Early Period

Haftarot

Simhat Torah   Joshua 1:1–18
Shelah-Lekha   Joshua 2:1–24
First Day of Passover   Joshua 5:2–6:1, 6:27

Moses is considered to be a super prophet. His successor, Joshua, is considered to be the first of the Prophets. The purpose of his book is to explain how the conquest of Canaan occurred and to pave the way for his succession.

The conquest of Canaan could not have occurred the way it was explained in the book even if we accept the biblical tradition that Canaan was forcibly seized by the Israelites.

How could semi-nomadic Israelite tribesmen, lacking any military history and only meagerly equipped with weapons, possibly overcome a much superior Canaanite foe who possessed more sophisticated technology and lived in walled cities?

Josephus attempted to answer this question by suggesting that the Israelites had acquired military equipment from the Egyptians who had drowned in the Red Sea. Unfortunately, it is a theory that doesn't hold much . . . water.

The Israelites' success in the face of Canaanite military superiority only becomes understandable when one considers certain factors that facilitated what appears to be a relatively rapid conquest of the country. Today, modern scholarship disagrees with this assumption and assumes the conquest might not have been a conquest at all, but rather an extended period of gradual settlement. However, if one just interprets from the text, it would appear that as a result of centuries of Egyptian exploitation, the mountainous areas in Canaan had left the people living there impoverished. They were a diverse group that lacked an ethnic commonality. This lack of ethnic connection hindered their city's armies from coming to the aid of another. As a result their political situation was always precarious.

At the same time, the Israelites, kindled by religious enthusiasm and newly formed national zeal, confronted a population that was unable to unite against the invader. Had another city's population rushed to the aid of Jericho at their hour of peril, the results would have been different.

A literal interpretation of the text would support a view that posited that Canaanite resistance was overcome by specific methods of warfare, which is clearly implied in the biblical stories. Supported by a highly developed intelligence system (the twelve spies), the attention to logistics, and the fact that Joshua prepared food and general supplies for the entire people prior to crossing the Jordan, as well as during the time of conquest, "the Israelites" were well prepared to conquer when they entered the land.

In order to overcome their military inferiority they continuously utilized deception, military cunning, and diversionary maneuvers, instead of engaging the enemy directly where chariots and a well-trained army would clearly prevail. The few times that an army actually fought another army, the Israelite forces were devastated.

Be-shallah
Judges 4:4–5:31

The surprise factor was decisive in major campaigns. Deborah, the Judge (haftarah Be-shallah Judges 4:4-5:31) who along with Barak confronted Sisera (who is said to have possessed nine hundred chariots), succeeded more by stealth and choice of time and place than as a result of superior forces. We are told the Israelite command held off the assault until the rainy season, when the Jezreel Valley became one large impassable swamp. This deprived the Canaanites of their mobility and eliminated the threat of their weapons of mass destruction. The book of Psalms 68:10 refers to Deborah's war taking place when the Kishon River was swollen (Judges 5:21). As a result, Sisera, the

4

Canaanite general, was forced to abandon his chariot, which was bogged down in mud, and forced to flee for his life on foot (Judges 4:7).

The book of Joshua is divided into two parts. The first part is concerned with the conquest and the nature of Joshua's leadership. It is organized geographically. The second part of the book is devoted to the distribution of the land to the tribes. The book was intended to serve as a reminder to future generations that God fulfills his promises. It reflects, through a number of incidents, the challenges the children of Israel confronted when they entered and attempted to conquer a more sophisticated civilization composed of a number of different peoples. These peoples lived in cities, had bronze weapons, and utilized horses when they went to war. Joshua's life and the conquest can be dated sometime in the 10th century, around 1150 B.C.E.

1150 B.C.E.

Three haftarot are excerpted from Joshua. These selections, in addition to their parallels to the Torah readings, were intended to demonstrate the transition of authority from Moses to Joshua. With the death of Joshua, the guiding influence of the haftarot truly began.

At the end of his book Joshua dies. Like his predecessor, Moses, and his ancestor Jacob, he assembles the host of Israel at Shechem and reminds them of their history and relationship to God. Like those who came before him, he establishes a covenant with the people and reminds them not to follow after other gods. This is recorded in a book of divine instruction.

The book of Joshua concludes with the death of Elazar, the son of Aaron, and notes that the bones of Joseph were buried at Shechem in the piece of ground that Jacob had bought from Hamor, Shechem's father. With the death of Joshua, a major period in the history of our people has come to a conclusion. The tribes have dispersed to lands they now claim, held together by a promise to aid one another in times of need. Joshua dies without appointing a successor. It is at this point that the period of the Judges commences.

Shechem

The Joshua Haftarot

Shelah-Lekha Joshua 2:1–24
This is one of the few passages in the Prophets that brilliantly parallels the Torah portion. In the Torah we read the story of the spies that Moses sent to spy out the land of Canaan, and in the book of Joshua we read about the spies sent to Jericho and the manner in which the Israelites conquered the city.

First Day of Passover Joshua 5:2-6:1–6:27
The haftarah commemorates the first Passover celebrated in the new land. It emphasizes the parallelisms with Moses, his predecessor. The crossing of the Jordan parallels the crossing of the Sea of Reeds. The celebration at Gilgal marks the entrance into the land in the same way that the Passover meal in Egypt marks the Exodus. On both occasions the hero is told he stands on holy ground and that his shoes need to be removed.

Simchat Torah Joshua 1:1–18
This haftarah emphasizes new beginnings. It details Joshua's new mission and his assumption of leadership.

■ ■ ■

Joshua was succeeded by the Judges. The way they functioned and the challenges they faced are the focus of the next unit.

Map 1 — Nexus 1 and 2
(Judges — Separation of 2 Kingdoms)

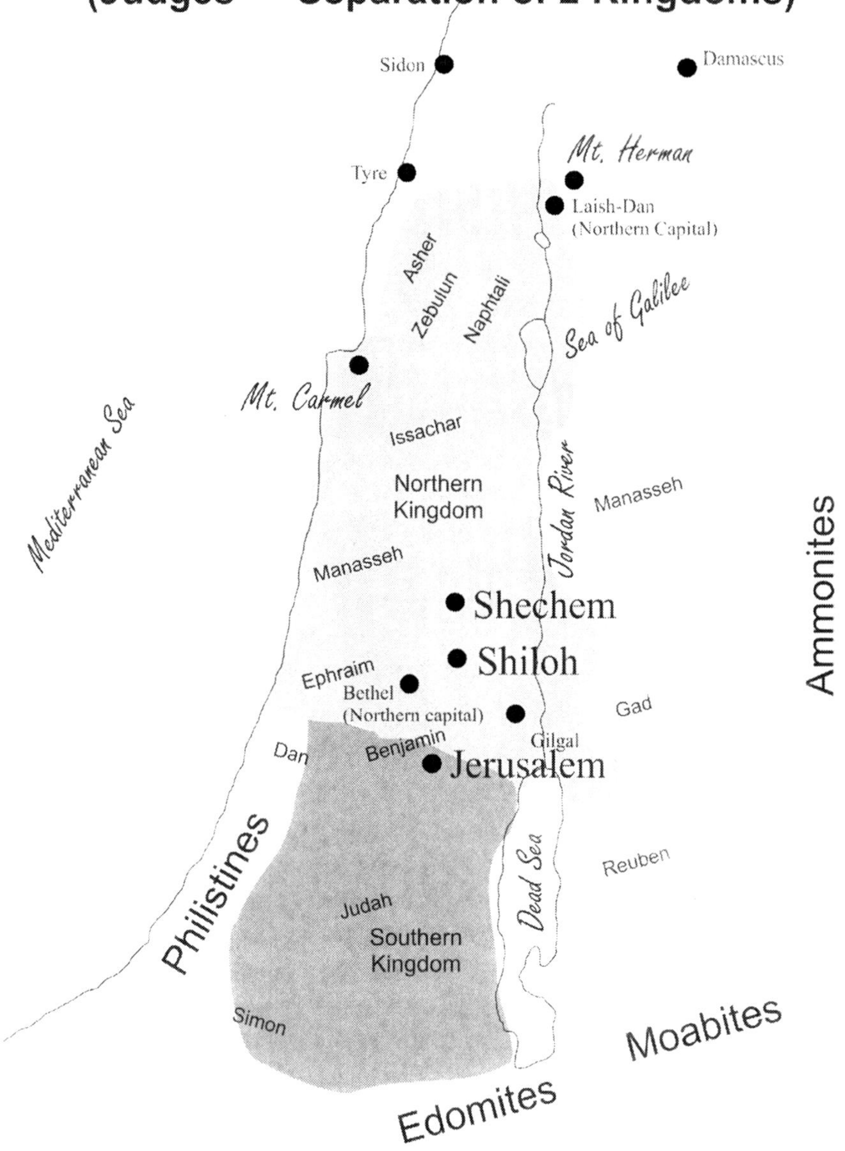

Sidon

Damascus

Mt. Herman

Tyre

Laish-Dan
(Northern Capital)

Asher

Zebulun

Naphtali

Sea of Galilee

Mt. Carmel

Mediterranean Sea

Issachar

Northern
Kingdom

Jordan River

Manasseh

Manasseh

Ammonites

● Shechem

● Shiloh

Ephraim

Bethel
(Northern capital)

Gad

Dan

Benjamin

Gilgal

● Jerusalem

Dead Sea

Reuben

Philistines

Judah

Southern
Kingdom

Simon

Moabites

Edomites

ISRAEL AND THE BATTLES FOUGHT BY THE JUDGES
(Northern and southern kingdoms are shaded differently.)

Enter the Judges

Who were the Judges? Could they try a case or have been on television?

The Judges were charismatic leaders and often military figures who stepped forward to overcome military threats that occurred after the death of Joshua and before the establishment of the monarchy. They were heroes. They were champions. They governed Israel for approximately one hundred and fifty years.

During a time of need, a Judge would simply appear, gather, and lead the people and then, in most instances, retire into the metaphoric sunset never to be heard of again. Their acts were considered to be "judgments" of the Lord. These heroes didn't come from any particular class or lineage and their status was not hereditary until the time of the last Judge, Samuel.

Joshua's death left the tribes without a unifying identifiable leader. As a result of their common historical experience, they remained bound together by what can be understood as an earlier version of the Confederation of States — that is to say they agreed to be governed by a series of loose covenants promising that one tribe would come to the aid of another in times of need.

The major charismatic Judges who delivered the people in times of distress were Othneil, Ehud, Gideon, Deborah, Jepthah and Samson. The last of the Judges was the priest, prophet, Judge, and kingmaker, Samuel. With the death of Samuel, the period of the Judges came to an end. This was around the year 1050 B.C.E.

1050 B.C.E.

Three portions from the book of Judges were selected to be haftarot. The first one is Be-shallah, which excerpts part of the story of Deborah. The second one is from Naso, which focuses on the circumstances surrounding the unusual birth of Samson. The third one corresponds to parshat Hukkat and is an expression of the need for a King.

Be-shallah
Naso

Be-shallah, Shabbat Shira (the Sabbath of Songs)
Judges 4:4–5:31
Parshat Be-shallah has songs in both the Torah and haftarah readings. Portions in the Torah and in the Prophets were written in a poetic form and reflect some of our most ancient texts. These texts were retained orally, perhaps musically, before they were transferred into writing. The Torah portion which extols in song God's victory at the Red Sea parallels the haftarah of the Song of Deborah.

Deborah's campaign marked the high point of national solidarity against foreign oppression. Her victory succeeded in uniting the tribe of Benjamin in the south to Naphtali in the north and largely undermined the Canaanite power structure in the north. Deborah led Israel's forces to victory, but her victory created a situation which opened the north to marauders from the desert. This situation persisted for a few generations and was only rectified during David's kingship.

A consequence of this victory was the strengthening of Israel's position in the Plain of Jezreel and the securing of a territorial connection between the tribes in Galilee in the north and those in the central region of the country.

Hukkat
Judges 11:1–33
The controversy and contention in the 11th century between Israelite and non-Israelite people in Gilead is reflected in the story of Jepthah. Jepthah was the son of a man from Gilead and a prostitute. He was scorned from birth, and when his siblings blocked his inheritance he fled and became the leader of a group of (there isn't a polite way to say this) thugs.

Jepthah's story is an early indication that the tribal confederacy wasn't providing sufficient defense against the neighboring tribes. His story was the first of many indications in the book of Judges that a different, more central form of government was needed. The Ammonites began to oppress the local villages and Jepthah, the only one with a private army, was approached by the people of Gilead, who asked him to lead them into battle. He

9

reminded them of the way they'd treated him in the past, and they in turn promised that if he were to prove victorious he would become their leader.

Jepthah's career began diplomatically. He visited the Amorites and asked, "To whom does the land really belong?" Eventually conversations and diplomatic attempts failed and Jepthah openly challenged and belittled Amorite leadership. He jeeringly claimed that the god of the Amorites couldn't protect his lands and the Ammonites should reconsider before starting a war. After all, the land in question hadn't really been theirs for 300 years! Of course the ramifications of who is the rightful owner of land in Israel has yet to be fully resolved, but that was not the focus of the text or of the haftarah.

Jepthah's negotiations failed, and prior to battle he uttered a vow that the first person to leave his house after he returned safely from battle would be sacrificed to the Lord. Like the Greek tragedies, the first person to cross his threshold was his only child.

The story illustrates the need for a community rationally governed by a king instead of being governed by spurious vows. The rabbis who selected this haftarah consciously omitted the end of the tale because they were creating parallels between the story of Moses, who solicits the Edomites and Amorites for permission to pass freely through their lands, and Jepthah, who was negotiating one of these tribe's descendants.

Naso

Birth of Samson and the struggle against the Philistines

Judges 13:2–35

This haftarah records the birth of the Judge named Samson. His birth, like that of Samuel which is read on the first day of Rosh Hashana, is heralded by an auspicious sign in the form of a woman's failure to become pregnant (reminiscent of Sarah and Rebecca), accompanied by a divine sign in either a vision or a special appearance of a man of God. In this case, our future hero is destined to serve as an instrument of God's judgment against the Philistines. But who were the Philistines?

10

The Philistines were a people who originated in Mycenaean Greece and migrated to Palestine and adapted to Canaanite culture. They clearly believed in Dagon, in whose honor they erected a sanctuary in Gaza. During the second half of the 12th century, they attained a level of military supremacy and replaced the Egyptians as the major force in Palestine. According to the Bible they were not united in a nation-state with a single ruler at their head, but had established a confederacy of city-states with a central sanctuary. Initially it appears that Gaza functioned as the focal point. The Philistines were technologically and militarily superior to the Canaanites and the Israelites.

Samson was from the tribe of Dan. His story, as problematic as it sounds, reflects one part of a greater conflict between the Philistines and the children of Israel.

NEXUS 2
THE ESTABLISHMENT OF THE DAVIDIC LINE

· ·

Samuel and his Influence: Judge, Priest, Prophet, and Kingmaker
From Judgeship to Monarchy
The Two Books of Samuel

Haftarot from 1 Samuel
Rosh Hashana day   1 Samuel 1:1–2:10
Shabbat Zachor   1 Samuel 15:2–34
Mahar Hodesh   1 Samuel 20:18–42
Korah   1 Samuel 11:14–12:22

While Samson represents the tribe of Dan's response to the Philistine incursion, the book of Judges indicates that several districts had already been conquered prior to Samson's gaining the tribes a brief respite. The decisive moment in the struggle between the Philistines and Israel occurred in the middle of the eleventh century in the Battle of Eben-ezer at Aphek when the tribes of the "house of Joseph," in the central hill country, were defeated by the
Shiloh   Philistines and their religious center, Shiloh, was destroyed.

Shiloh is one of those words that is associated with the Bible but for some reason is never explained. Shiloh served as the primary (not the sole) national religious center, where the ark and the holy sanctuary were housed. It was the seat of the priestly house of Eli. It was the place where Samuel's mother came to pray for a child, and it was the place where Israelites went for festivals and convocations. When the Philistines captured the Ark of the Covenant, it symbolized the subjugation of the entire tribal confederacy of Israel. It predated the establishment of Jerusalem as a holy city.

It was at this juncture, when the future of Israel was imperiled, that redemption occurred in the guise of Samuel, the prophet, Judge, priest, and eventually kingmaker. It was he who revived the people's waning spirits and led the way to national liberation.

Who was Samuel?
Samuel was a priest; the haftarah read on the first day of Rosh Hashana testifies that his life was dedicated to God (1 Samuel 1:1-2:10). He was a Judge and his sons served as Judges in Beersheba. His sphere of influence encompassed the territories of Benjamin and Ephraim, which at the time, were under constant attack from the Philistines. He was a prophet and is described as the head of the prophetic guild, also known as "sons of the prophet." This guild helped to stimulate the needed national awakening, the defense against the Philistines, and most likely laid the groundwork for the establishment of the monarchy. Samuel's story is so detailed that two books in the Prophetic canon, including four haftarot in the first book of Samuel, and two from the second, are devoted to him.

. . . .

Interlude: Enter the Prophets

What is a prophet and what did they do? One common assumption about prophets is that they heard the word of the Lord. What exactly does that mean?

The earliest words used to describe a prophet were "roeh," which means "a person who sees," and "hozeh," "one who has visions." The only person in our tradition who actually spoke to the Lord and saw some aspect of the Lord was Moses. We can consider him kind of a super prophet.

The prophets who followed him didn't have the same access. They, to use a term coined by Michael Fishbane in his haftarah commentary, saw or heard the message of the Lord *through a glass darkly.* In other words, the communication between them and God was cloudy. The only example of a prophecy in the Torah is the story of the non-Israelite prophet, Billam.

One can assume that prophecy in ancient Israel began with **1150 B.C.E.** Joshua around 1150 B.C.E. There were many kinds of

13

prophets. Some travelled in groups. Some were prophets to kings and others were individuals, who for some reason, were called to prophecy.

Some of the early prophets were miracle workers. Others were public reformers who stood up and challenged the religious and political establishments of the times. Some of them were priests, others (well, we don't know very much about this period, or about why they were called, if they were called, or how they were called) we just have words and books that were recorded in their names. Elijah and Elisha were prominent figures in the period of the early monarchy, 900-830s, and other prophets like Jeremiah and Ezekiel lived hundreds of years later.

Elijah
Elisha
Jeremiah
Ezekiel

In order to obtain a fuller picture of their efforts, one needs to read the stories recorded in their names. These stories provide a more extensive vision of the roles they played than is recorded in the haftarot. Elijah and Elisha, for example, did more than just perform miracles. They challenged the monarchical establishment! Elisha actually anointed one of the northern kings' generals as king! This was more than just chutzpah; it was actively initiating rebellion!

The institution of prophecy began around the year 1150 B.C.E. and came to an end after the Second Temple was rebuilt some 690 years later.

Approximately one hundred and fifty years after the death of Joshua, the book of Judges informs the reader that a more effective form of government was needed. The people called for a king. It was the decision and responsibility of the last of the Judges, a man who was also a priest and a prophet, to step into the role of kingmaker. This was Samuel, the man responsible for the anointing of the first two kings, Saul and David. The time of his judgeship coincides with the appearance of prophets in our literature.

There were major prophets and minor prophets. Isaiah, Jeremiah, and Ezekiel are considered to be major prophets. This is because their books are the three largest prophetic compilations in our tradition. Isaiah lived approximately one hundred years before Jeremiah and Ezekiel. The minor prophets have smaller books.

Jeremiah prophesied in Judah from the 13th year of Josiah (627 B.C.E.) to the 11th year of Zedekiah (586 B.C.E.). I know we haven't discussed Zedekiah but don't worry, we will. Jeremiah lived in a time when Judah had lost its national independence and was controlled first by the Egyptians, and then by the Babylonians. Jeremiah also lived through the period of the first and second forced exiles. It was during the second exile that the Temple, Jerusalem, and the province of Judah were destroyed. Did I say first and second exiles? Whoops! More about that later.

■ ■ ■

Prophecy continued in Babylon after the death of Ezekiel. This was the period when the last three prophets, Haggai, Zechariah, and Malachi, prophesied. With the death of Malachi, Jewish life changed dramatically and the basis for what evolved into modern Jewish life began to emerge. What that is, and how we arrived at that point, will be summarized much, much later.

....

Samuel, once again

In order to fully understand the haftarot excerpted from the first book of Samuel, it is important to understand the history and the politics leading up to the anointing of Saul and the subsequent anointing of David as the second king of Israel.

The first book of Samuel begins with a summary of the unusual circumstances surrounding his birth. The initial part of the book stresses the need for a king and how Samuel selects and positions Saul to be accepted as king. The book details Saul's initial successes and then relates a series of incidents that lead to Samuel rejecting Saul and shifting his allegiance to David, whom he appoints to be Saul's successor.

Imagine Saul's reaction to having his prophet withdraw his support and appoint someone else in his stead. And while he was still the ruling king! If it were me, I would have been incensed and would certainly feel threatened. Imagine how Saul reacted when he heard the people chant, "Saul has killed thousands and David ten thousands."

Suffice it to say, the first book of Samuel details a jealous Saul actively pursuing David with the intent of eliminating his rival. Towards the end of the book Samuel dies and the book concludes with the death of Saul and his three sons.

Saul was described as a brave soldier, a man of the people. It is possible that the text described him in this manner to highlight his characteristics or to distinguish him from the ways the authors understood the Canaanite kings of the time. If Israel had to have a king, bottom line, he would be accessible. He was of course (he had to be) a charismatic leader rooted in the period and tradition of the Judges.

Gilgal

Saul (1079–1007) first emerged as a military leader. One of his first acts was to come to the rescue of Jabesh-Gilead, the Transjordanian city whose inhabitants were related to his tribe, the Benjaminites (Judges 21:8). He defeated the Ammonites and as a consequence was crowned at Gilgal (1 Sam 11:15).

Parshat Korah

The selected haftarah corresponding to parshat Korah (1 Samuel 11:14–12:22) highlights the end of the Judges' regional leadership and the beginning of the monarchy. The haftarah focuses on the coronation of Saul as the first king of Israel. He was anointed by Samuel but it wasn't, at least initially, an act that Samuel desired. Earlier in the story Samuel admonishes the people for desiring a king and challenges them to have faith in God instead. *"You shall cry out in that day because of your king whom you have chosen and the Lord will not hear you"* (1 Sam 8:18). His challenge was rejected. The monarchy was created almost as a concession to the people of Israel.

Following Saul's initial victory, he directed his efforts at Israel's main enemies, the Philistines (1 Sam 14:46–7). At one point he was engaging enemies on every front: the

16

Moabites, the Ammonites, the Edomites, the Zobahites, and the Philistines. He introduced major military innovations by creating a standing army organized on the basis of traditional tribal and geographical structure.

For example, all the sons of Jesse (David's father) served in the same army unit (1 Sam 17:18). As a result of his innovations, a new class of people emerged who had a special relationship to the king. Let's call them "nobles." Saul granted them estates and exempted them from mandatory tithes. His reign was a period of transition between the tribal and patriarchal systems to a monarchial one that became more fully implemented during the reigns of David and Solomon.

The final period of his reign was marked by the struggle between his increasingly tyrannical attitude (his desire to kill David) and the traditional leadership that had formerly ruled the land. Saul was a Macbeth-type figure, torn and tragic and unable to meet or rise to the occasions that the times demanded. The book of Samuel is heavily weighted against Saul. The historian Ben-Sasson suggests that Saul's story was most likely put into its final form by a pro-David faction.

The haftarah that is read on the Sabbath before Purim **Shabbat Zachor** (Shabbat Zachor; 1 Samuel 15:2–34) illustrates one of the incidents that resulted in Samuel's removing the mantle of leadership from Saul and placing it upon the shoulders of the rising star, David.

Saul was instructed by Samuel to eliminate Agag, king of the Amalekites, and all of his family. Saul follows Samuel's orders but chooses not to kill Agag. As a result Samuel and Saul quarrel. Samuel announces God rejected him as king because he failed to fulfill God's desires. Imagine that! Samuel anointed him and then changed his mind and took it away!

Saul, perhaps not wanting to lose Samuel's support, apologized and the two of them went to the shrine at Gilgal **Gilgal** where Samuel had Agag brought forth and slaughtered him himself.

It is possible that the struggle for power between Saul and David, which is played out in the haftarah Mahar Hodesh, led the Philistines to believe that the time to strike the final blow against Saul and his kingdom had finally arrived.

The Philistines employed a completely new strategy. They sent their armies to the weakest point in Saul's kingdom, the remnants of the Canaanite cities, in the Jezreel and Beth-Shean valleys, where they could take advantage of their military superiority. This forced Saul to engage them from a position of military weakness at Gilboah. Saul was defeated and as a result, the kingdom split in two. The area across the Jordan and in the mountains remained faithful to Saul's son, Ish-bosheth, and his general, Abner, while the south supported David. David, for reasons soon to be shared, was eventually appointed king of Judah.

The third haftarah selection is concerned with King Saul and the future King David. It appears in our liturgical cycle when Shabbat falls on the day before the beginning of the new month. This is called Mahar Hodesh, or the day before the new month. The selection is read as a haftarah because the text mentions the "new month."

For simplicity sake, let's assume we can divide David's life into four stages. The first was his emergence as the simple son of Jesse of Bethlehem, the boy who defeated Goliath. As a result of this victory and his humility, he appears at Saul's court, is praised for his deeds, and eventually marries Saul's younger daughter, Michal. Saul originally attempted to marry David to an older daughter, but let's just say it didn't work out.

As David's popularity grew, so did Saul's jealousy. Saul's jealousy and the ways David responded are encapsulated in the second stage of David's life. The haftarah called Mahar Hodesh provides insight into the tensions that were occurring between David and an increasingly jealous Saul.

These tensions are further developed in 1 Samuel chapters 16–27. We are told that David escapes from Saul on numerous occasions and attracts increasingly large numbers of supporters. Initially he began with thirty men, which eventually grew to six hundred. Surprisingly, our text indicates that the men were generally landless, vain, and of questionable honor. To state it bluntly, David did not initially find support from his own clan and was forced to enlist a different sort of group. Our glorious and noble leader was, at least initially, anything but that.

....

David the King
Myth and Reality

Haftarot from 2 Samuel
Shemini 2 Samuel 6:1–7:17
7th day of Passover 2 Samuel 22:1–51
Ha'azinu (between Yom HaKippurim and Sukkot)
    2 Samuel 22:1–51

Introduction
Fortunately more information is available about the Davidic court than any other period of Israelite rule. Like other great kingdoms of the ancient Near East, David employed scribes trained to record the many needs of a growing and prosperous state. David's story is unique in the historical literature of the ancient Near East because the author of his book adds a new dimension to his developing biography: a moral standard.

For example, David is depicted as having committed a grievous sin when he sent Uriah the Hittite to his death, thus enabling him to marry Uriah's wife, Bat Sheva. This type of honesty was, up until this point, unknown in the literature of the time. Similarly, his family difficulties, including the murder of his son Amnon and the revolt of another son, Absalom, are regarded as divine punishments.

If one studies the history of David's rise to power and rule, one finds the moral quality of his life to be lacking. The fact that his chronicler acknowledged these faults and flaws added a new dimension to how religious leadership was perceived. The implications of these literary innovations

19

allowed generations to identify, understand, and wrestle with themselves to be better human beings.

The third stage in David's life occurred when, in order not to be killed by Saul, he allied and collaborated with the Philistines and became a protégé of Achish, King of Gath. This forced David to balance his dual loyalties to the Philistines and to the elders of the clans of southern Judah. As a result of Saul's defeat and death at Gibeah, the ties between Judah (the south) and the northern tribes weakened. David seized the moment and settled his entire force in Hebron (Judah), thus creating a difficult situation for the elders of Judah, who desired to keep themselves separate from the other tribes but at the same time desired protection against the Philistines. They were caught between a rock and a hard place, and in what I suspect was an act of desperation they decided to crown David king. This brings us to the fourth stage of David's life.

Hebron David was crowned at Hebron. He held power for seven years and six months before bitter fighting broke out between Abner, Saul's general, and Ishboshet, Saul's son, both of whom were supported by the northern tribes. Abner acted as the regent of what remained of Saul's kingdom and entered into an agreement with David guaranteeing David's kingship of the north if he displaced David's current general, Joab (2 Samuel 3:27–39). David must have acquiesced because Joab and Ishboshet were assassinated shortly afterwards and Abner succeeded in his stead. As a result of this alliance, David, the only one capable of leading an army against the Philistines, became king of Judah and Israel.

**Three haftarot are excerpted from
the 2nd book of Samuel**

Shemini
2 Samuel 6:1–7:17
The haftarah for parshat Shemini takes place after the death of King Saul. David was recently crowned king in Hebron. He proceeded to conquer Jerusalem and defeat the **1000 B.C.E.** Philistines. It is around 1000 B.C.E. In order to unite his kingdom he seeks to make Jerusalem the nation's capital. He brings the ark to Jerusalem from Shiloh, where it had

20

been kept since earlier wars with the Philistines. The transfer of the ark to the ancient site of Jebus (Jerusalem) was designed to unite the tribes of Israel (north) and Judah (south) around a sacred center. David also expanded Israel beyond the framework of Canaan, conquering Edom and Moab. He established treaties with Tyre and Sidon and paved the way for Solomon's rule.

7th day of Passover
2 Samuel 22:1–51
It is customary to recite David's song of Thanksgiving, which parallels the Song of the Sea which is read on the 7th day of Passover, and to also read it when parshat Ha'azinu falls between Yom Ha Kippurim and Sukkot. This haftarah is referred to as David's great hymn of victory and thanksgiving which he sang to God after being saved from "the hands of Saul." One would have thought it should have been part of the first book of Samuel, since that was when the incident occurred. But the authors of the books of Samuel chose to place it near the end of the book so it could serve as a fitting testimonial to a great military hero who at the end of his life thanked God. Just as Moses chants a final song before he dies, so too did David.

Ha'azinu falls between Yom Ha Kippurim and Sukkot

■ ■ ■

David was succeeded by his son Solomon.

David's Legacy and Solomon the Wise, or was he?

Haftarot from 1 Kings

Hayyei Sarah	1 Kings 1:1–31	David old, Solomon king
Miketz	1 Kings 3:15–4:1	965 B.C.E., start of Solomon's reign
Vayehi	1 Kings 2:1–12	David's last will and testament
Terumah	1 Kings 5:26–6:13	Solomon beginning of construction
Ki Tissa	1 Kings 18:1–39	Elijah at Mt. Carmel
Vayakhel	1 Kings 7:40–50	Building Temple
Pekudei	1 Kings 7:51–8:21	Temple's completion and moving ark
Pinhas (prior to 17 Tammuz)	1 Kings 18:46–19:21	Elijah post–Mt. Carmel
2nd Shabbat Hanukkah	1 Kings 7:40–50	Hiram and Solomon
Sukkoth day 2	1 Kings 8:2–21	Solomon moving ark
Shemini Atzeret	1 Kings 8:54–66	Solomon

Transition of power

Period before building of the Temple.

Eleven haftarot were excerpted from the first book of Kings. All are concerned with either the death of King David or the manner in which Solomon, David's son and successor, established his throne and built and dedicated the Temple. This is one of the larger groups of haftarot relating to a specific period in prophetic history. Clearly the rabbis living twelve hundred years later understood how formative and important it was to reinforce the importance of the Davidic dynasty. These eleven haftarot focus on the transition of power and the circumstances leading up to the building of the Temple.

Haftarot from 2 Kings

Va-yera	2 Kings 4:1–37	Elisha the miracle man
Tazria	2 Kings 4:42–5:19	Elisha the miracle man
Metzora	2 Kings 7:3–20	The story of the lepers

Shabbat Shekalim	2 Kings 12:1–17	Jehoash partially cleans house
Passover day 2	2 Kings 23:1–9, 21–25	Josiah reads the scroll

The books of Kings are divided into three sections. The first section summarizes the circumstances of Solomon's ascent to the throne and describes the source of his wisdom, his reign over the United Kingdom of Israel, and his great building plan. The second section is concerned with the circumstances surrounding the beginnings of the rejection of his authority by the northern tribes. The third and final section describes the Davidic dynasty in Judah, the Southern Kingdom, leading up to Babylonia's conquering of Judea and destroying Jerusalem and the Temple in 586 B.C.E.

The books of Kings

586 B.C.E.

In order to more fully understand these haftarot it is necessary to review the accomplishments and last days of David, the poet, king, and man, who in spite of his behavior (which was less than exemplary), established an enduring covenant between God and the Jewish people. David is considered to be the progenitor of the Messiah. The Talmud claims he authored many of the Psalms, and our literature depicts him as the ideal ruler. Historically we know that was hardly the case. The David extolled in our liturgy bears little resemblance to the historical David.

I think David's greatest accomplishment and that which enabled him to establish a dynasty was the way he intertwined theology with politics. While today, many of us might find the intermingling of religion and politics inappropriate and undesirable, in David's world it was an effective and innovative strategy. It could be that David's chroniclers were the ones responsible for this linkage.

David's first kingly act was to publicly reenact the covenantal ceremony that Moses made with God at Sinai. *"I have made a covenant with my chosen. I have sworn unto David my servant. Thy seed will I establish for ever."* (Psalm 89:3–4).

23

This simple act of spiritual affirmation equated kingly status with near priestly sanctity. The king spiritually became linked to the holy city where God would dwell. According to the book of Samuel, David's sons, as a result of their birth, were also empowered to serve in a priestly capacity. This special sanctity provided two of his sons, Adonijah and Absalom, with the ability to later rally support when they rebelled against their father.

His second act was to secretly arrange for the death of anyone in Saul's household who could potentially threaten his kingdom.

He was an excellent general. His military and political maneuvering united the northern and southern tribes. Unfortunately, it was a charisma-based unification rather than one which could endure on its own. David sought to weaken the influence of the tribes by creating a class of bureaucrats loyal only to him. This angered tribal leadership who represented the elders of Israel and continued to cause him and Solomon trouble throughout their reigns.

When David's charismatic ability diminished, a series of rebellions led by people who sought a return to the old ways occurred. In one instance David was forced to flee for his life, and in order to regain his power he was forced to ally with the men of Judah. In return for their loyalty they were exempted from paying taxes. This strategic alliance further alienated David from the northern tribes. A third revolt broke out led by a Benjaminite (remember King Saul was a Benjaminite) named Sheba ben Bichri.

Hayyei Sarah In an attempt to end the rebellions, David proclaimed Solomon, the son of his favorite wife, Bathsheba, to be his successor. These are the circumstances that led up to the haftarah for Hayyei Sarah.

Vayehi The haftarah from parashat Vayehi (1 Kings 2:1–12), which is read nine weeks later, brings David's story to a conclusion. In that text he delivers to his son Solomon the wisdom he has accumulated throughout his life in a manner reminiscent of Moses' last speech. In that speech, David, conscious of his approaching death, advises Solomon what

24

needs to be done if he wishes to retain his kingship. His advice can be understood in one of two ways. Either it is a fine blend of political and spiritual wisdom or it reflects the experiences of an angry and vengeful man. It is 965 B.C.E. and Solomon has just become king.

965 B.C.E.

....

Solomon the Wise, or was he?

Haftaraot

Miketz	1 Kings 3:15–4:1	The wise king
Terumah	1 Kings 5:26–6:13	Temple construction
Vayakhel	1 Kings 7:40–50	Temple architect
Pekudei-Vayakhel		
	1 Kings 7:40–50	Construction completed
Shabbat Hanukkah (2)		
	1 Kings 7:40–50	Hiram and Solomon
Second day Sukkoth		
	1 Kings 8:2–21	Solomon moves the ark
Shemini Atzeret		
	1 Kings 8:54–66	Solomon ends the festival

Solomon reigned from 965–928 B.C.E. He is credited with being a wise king and the father of wisdom in Israel.

965–928 B.C.E.

> "And Solomon's wisdom excelled the wisdom of all the children of the east county, and all the wisdom of Egypt. For he was wiser than all men . . . And his spake three thousand proverbs; and his sons were a thousand and five . . . And there came of all people to hear the Wisdom of Solomon . . ." (1 Kings 4:30–34)

The haftarah for Miketz establishes Solomon as a wise king. He dreams in a manner reminiscent of the patriarch Joseph and establishes himself as a person gifted with wisdom. He dreams of going to Jerusalem and standing before the Ark of the Covenant, thus reenforcing the centrality of Jerusalem, the place where God's Temple will be built.

Miketz

Terumah,
Vayakhel-
Pekudei,
second Shabbat
of Hanukkah
958 B.C.E.
The dream sets the stage for the haftarot which coincide with the following parshiot Terumah, Vayakhel-Pekudei, and the second Shabbat of Hanukkah. It is 958 B.C.E.

During his long and peaceful reign, the united Israel became a great and wealthy kingdom. Its influence spread throughout the ancient world. Israel, during that period, was recognized as the leading nation-state between Egypt and Asia Minor. Solomon's marriage to "the daughter of Pharaoh" is evidence of this high standing.

The Kingdom of Solomon included all David's conquests: Edom, Moab, Ammon, and Aram-Damascus. He was the sole ruler over the chief trade routes connecting Mesopotamia and Syria to Egypt. He controlled the Arabian trade which mainly transported spices, myrrh, and frankincense. The spices and other luxuries originated in south Arabia (Sheba) and were in great demand in the courts of Syria and Mediterranean rulers. The increasing importance of Solomon's kingdom in international trade and the economic progress that resulted created close bonds between Israel and neighboring states, particularly with Tyre, the largest trade center on the Phoenician coast. Solomon supplied Hiram with agricultural surplus and in return received the raw materials he needed for his buildings, particularly cedar wood. It was a perfect match!

Vayakhel
1 Kings 7:40–50
Vayakhel-
Pekudei
1 Kings 7:40–50
2nd Shabbat of
Hanukkah
The haftarot that are read corresponding to parshat Vayakhel, 1 Kings 7:40–50, and Vayakhel-Pekudei, 1 Kings 7:40–50, and the 2nd Shabbat of Hanukkah reflect Solomon and Hiram's relationship. The two of them established a venture, without intermediaries, that transported luxury goods (ivory, gold, rare woods, rare beasts and birds). The collection of rare animals for a royal zoo was an established monarchical custom in the courts of Assyrian kings from the eleventh to ninth centuries.

As a result of his relationship with Hiram, Israel gained access to northern Syria and neighboring countries that had the needed metals necessary for the Temple's construction. Solomon imported copper from Cyprus and iron from Asia Minor. The long period of peace also gave impetus to improved means of production. Ploughs with iron blades appeared, which enlarged the areas being cultivated. The increased cultivation of the land resulted in agricultural excess which were exported to other nations.

Finally, a clear sign of economic progress was the widespread building which took place across the land. Cities were fortified according to a uniform architectural style, but the greatest innovation took place in Jerusalem. Solomon physically transformed Jerusalem into a royal city and a temple city in accordance with David's design, thus making the capital the kingdom's religious center.

The establishment of a Temple in a city devoid of tribal traditions created opposition from the old religious centers that still played a vital role in the people's lives. Solomon had the Ark of the Covenant transported to Jerusalem (this is chronicled in the haftarah for the Second day Sukkoth, Kings 1, 8:2–21) and formally dedicated the Temple after it had been completed. (This is reflected in the haftarah for Shemini Atzeret). What appeared to be a significant religious act had huge political consequences. It is possible that the religious dissatisfaction with Jerusalem could have been one of the main factors behind the revolt that broke out after Solomon's death.

Second day
Sukkoth
Kings 1, 8:2–21

Shemini Atzeret

How wise was he really?
Solomon suffered from visions of grandeur. In order to implement the large-scale building effort that he envisioned and particularly the construction of the Temple, workers needed to be recruited and taxes needed to be imposed on the people. This was a huge undertaking: the chronicler informs us that 80,000 people worked in the quarries and were supervised by 3,300 officers. These details are found in haftarah Terumah.

Terumah

These measures were not well received and resulted in a bitterness that in due course fostered a rebellion. The expense of providing supplies for the royal court and army that was primarily stationed in and around Jerusalem forced Solomon to impose a second levy (tax). One can assume that the reception of this new tax also wasn't joyously accepted. What a surprise!

The texts selected to serve as haftarot aggrandized Solomon's early years and reflect the summit of this nexus point. He was portrayed as the builder of the Temple and the ruler in whose days Judah and Israel were as numerous *as the sand which is by the sea in multitude, eating and drinking, and making merry* (1 Kings 4:20).

The rabbis, looking backward twelve hundred years later, understood or at least taught that peace, security, and prosperity were a result of virtuous and wise leadership and a government that followed God's ways.

What were they drinking?

Towards the end of Solomon's reign the international picture changed and the subsequent difficulties that occurred were explained as a punishment for allowing his alien wives to introduce idolatrous cults in the court (1 Kings 11:14).

945 B.C.E.   What actually happened was that in the year 945 B.C.E., a new dynasty emerged in Egypt which was hostile to Solomon and sought to weaken Israel's influence in the ancient world. They successfully encouraged rebellions and breakaways in the extremities of Solomon's kingdom. The establishment of new independent kingdoms weakened Israel economically, diminished Israel's markets, and restricted its control of the trade routes. Israel's balance of trade shifted from a positive balance of trade to a negative one. In order to pay his debts to Hiram for the needed raw materials, Solomon was forced to cede control of twenty cities from Acco in the south to Tyre in the north.

It is against this background that a revolt against
928 B.C.E.   Rehoboam, Solomon's son, occurred in 928 B.C.E. This rebellion resulted in the separation of Judah in the south from what would be called Israel in the north. The division into two kingdoms reflects the end of the second nexus and sets the stage for the creation of the third nexus point which came to a conclusion two hundred years later. It appears that the failure to integrate tribal and pre-Temple religious traditions was the Achilles' heel of the monarchy. This issue is not reflected in the rabbis' understanding and interpretation of this period. Perhaps it was overshadowed by the traumatic realization that the disappearance of the Northern Kingdom contained haunting lessons.

Map 2 — Nexus 3
930–722 B.C.E.
Assyria conquers Israel

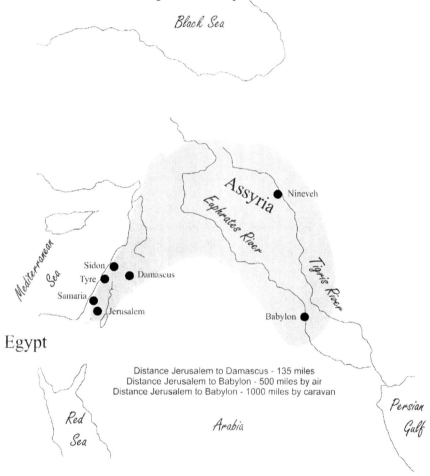

Black Sea

Assyria

Nineveh

Euphrates River

Tigris River

Mediterranean Sea

Sidon

Tyre

Samaria

Damascus

Jerusalem

Babylon

Egypt

Distance Jerusalem to Damascus - 135 miles
Distance Jerusalem to Babylon - 500 miles by air
Distance Jerusalem to Babylon - 1000 miles by caravan

Red Sea

Arabia

Persian Gulf

NEXUS 3

TWO KINGDOMS DIVIDED

••

Two Centuries of Lessons Learned

Haftarot from Kings (continued)
The Elijah and Elisha stories

Va'era	2 Kings 4:1–37	Elisha
Ki Tissa	1 Kings 18:1–139	Elijah and prophets of Baal 871–852 B.C.E.
Tazria	2 Kings 4:42–5:19	Elisha 851–842
Metzora	2 Kings 7:3-20	Elisha
Pinhas	1 Kings 18:46–19:21	Elijah

928 B.C.E.

722 B.C.E.

The second section of the books of Kings begins with the separation of Israel into two kingdoms. This occurred in 928 B.C.E. From this point onward the books of Kings tell the overlapping histories of the kings of Judah and Israel. This covers a period of almost two centuries until the Northern Kingdom was destroyed by Assyria in 722 B.C.E. The circumstances leading up to the dissolution of the Northern Kingdom are the focus of the third nexus point.

Background

Shechem

Solomon might have been a wise leader and a great builder, but he could have been a better planner. History emulates his greatness but neglects to inform us that he left a weakened overtaxed country committed to a series of unfair treaties with obvious bias towards the tribe of Judah who dwelt in the south. This unfair treatment angered the northern tribes. When Rehoboam, Solomon's son, ascended the throne in 928 B.C.E., resistance to the monarchy had never been greater. The tribes of Israel demanded that the coronation take place at the ancient site of Shechem instead of Jerusalem. The situation was serious enough that Rehoboam acquiesced.

The book of Kings portrays Rehoboam as being poorly advised and attempting to rule both the north and the south with an iron hand.

"My father chastised you with whips, but I will chastise you with scorpions." (1 Kings 12:11)

However, the split occurred with a minimum amount of violence. This was most likely because Rehoboam was concerned that Shishak, the new ruler of Egypt, was encouraging a former employee of Solomon, to lead a rebellion. This individual was named Jeroboam and at one time he was in charge of the forced labor crews in Jerusalem. We are informed in 1 Kings 11:30-31 that the prophet Ahijah came to him and foretold that ten of the twelve tribes would be taken from the descendants of Solomon and given to him.

And he said to Jeroboam, Take for yourself ten pieces; for thus says the Lord, the God of Israel, "Behold I will tear the kingdom out of the hand of Solomon and give you ten tribes.

Solomon responded to this prophecy by calling for his death. Jeroboam fled to Egypt and remained there until the death of Solomon. With the backing of Egypt he led a revolt that successfully attracted all of the tribes with the exception of Judah and Benjamin. Judah and Benjamin were situated in the south. Jeroboam called his country *Israel*, which came to be known in the 7th century as *Ephraim*. Israel, Ephraim, or the Northern Kingdom existed from approximately 930-721 B.C.E.   **930–721** B.C.E.

■ ■ ■

Judah's history for the next sixty years can be mostly described as an attempt to reestablish its authority over the Northern Kingdom (930-870 B.C.E.). Following that the geopolitics of the ancient world changed and the next eighty years resulted in a period of friendly alliances where both nations cooperated against common enemies, specifically Damascus (870-800 B.C.E.).

Jeroboam and the creation of the Northern Kingdom

The process of creating a country is a complicated one. Jeroboam was a king with a problem. The Temple was in Jerusalem and Jerusalem was in Judah. Where and how would his people worship?

In response to this situation Jeroboam created two centers of worship, one on the northern border and one even farther north on the slopes of Mount Hermon. The first site, *Beth El*, the place where Jacob had his vision of a ladder reaching up to heaven, was twelve miles north of Jerusalem. The second site was a Canaanite city north of the Sea of Galilee on the slopes of Mount Hermon called *Laish*. Jeroboam renamed it Dan and established a religious center with its own Levitical priesthood descended from Moses (Judges 18:30). At each of these locations a golden calf was erected.

Jeroboam was succeeded by Nadab (910–909 B.C.E.), who was assassinated by Baasha (909–886 B.C.E.), who was succeeded by Elah (886–885 B.C.E.), who was assassinated by one of his captains named Zimri (885 B.C.E.). Zimri held on to the throne for seven days and then committed suicide when he learned that the army had declared their commanding general, Omri, to be their new king.

Omri reestablished the Northern Kingdom by appointing priests from non-Levite families and encouraging the construction of local places of sacrifice. He also permitted the worship of other gods. It is 928 B.C.E.

928 B.C.E.

One of Omri's first acts as king was to arrange a strategic alliance with the king of Phoenicia by marrying his son Ahab to Jezebel, a priestess of the god Baal. Much of the prophetic activity for the next two centuries was directed against the Northern Kingdom which came to be called Samaria. The activity of the prophet Elijah and his disciple Elisha takes place during this period. The actors, for the most part, are Elijah, Ahab, Jezebel, and Elisha. This is the period that roughly spans 871–842 B.C.E.

Ahab
Jezebel

Samaria

871–842 B.C.E.

This is the background for the haftarot for Pinhas and Ki Tissa. The haftarot reflect Elisha's (Elijah's disciple) ministry. The haftarot of Va'era, Tazria, and Metzora also take place during this period.

Pinhas
Ki Tissa
Va'era
Tazria
Metzora

The stories of Elisha at first glance appear to be a collection of folk tales that focus on his faith and wonder-working powers. However, both Elijah and Elisha and the "Band of Prophets" were active political forces. The haftarah for Tazria takes place when Israel's (Samaria) influence was at its weakest. The reference to the king of Israel being ordered to cure Naaman, the Aram general, of leprosy was indicative of the Northern Kingdom's vassalage to Aram.

Tazria

The close economic and military ties between Israel and the Syro-Phoenician states, particularly Tyre, resulted in Syro-Phoenican culture and religion being accepted in Israel. A Temple to Baal, where Tyrian priests officiated, was erected in Samaria. One could assume that extensive groupings of the upper classes, such as state officials and courtiers, followed the royal lead. Portions of the first book of Kings highlight Jezebel's (the daughter-in-law of Omri) disregard for Israelite customs when she seized the vineyard of Naboth, the Jezreelite, and was supported by the king. This act was condemned by Elijah and reveals the tension between the prophets and the ruling class. This conflict reached its zenith in another prophetic incident which takes place between Elijah and the queen's prophets on Mount Carmel. That is the subject of the haftarah for Ki Tissa.

Ki Tissa

Elijah defeats the prophets of Baal, but he and the "sons of the prophets" lacked sufficient strength to overthrow the queen. Jezebel retaliated and began to persecute the prophets. Obadiah, a contemporary prophet, hides some of the fleeing members of the prophetic guild from Jezebel's persecution. While Obadiah can be placed in this period, a disagreement exists regarding when the book was completed and to what period it can be associated. The Sephardic tradition selected Obadiah chapter 1:1-21 to be the haftarah for Va-yishlah primarily because of its relationship to the prophetic collections of Joel, who was Amos' predecessor. Obadiah preaches that divine judgment will be directed at Edom. Later in his book he prophesied that God would dwell once again in Zion. This latter

Obadiah

Va-yishlah

Joel

33

prophecy led many to believe the book was written or edited after the destruction of the Temple in 586 B.C.E.; the former connects it with the period of Elijah and Elisha.

In time the prophetic guild gained strength and was openly able to oppose the policies of the royal family. This was the mission of Elijah's disciple, Elisha. The increasingly open resistance to royal policies was one of the reasons for the collapse of the Omrid dynasty in 842 B.C.E. The second book of Kings (2 Kings 9) recounts the story of Elisha inspiring and anointing one of the Omri's grandsons' generals, a man named Jehu, to revolt against Jehoram the son of Ahaz, the grandson of Omri.

Shabbat Shekalim 2 Kings 12:1-17
This haftarah shifts to Judah (the Southern Kingdom) and explains how a priest, Jehoida, established Jehoash, who had been hidden in the House of the Lord during the reign of Queen Athaliah, as king. Athaliah was also a worshipper of Baal. Apparently a revolt took place and the Temple of Baal and its priesthood were destroyed, but the shrines were not removed and some of the people continued worshiping Baal. The text informs us that Jehoash was a good king who ruled for forty years. In a sense he was a precursor to Hezekiah and Josiah, who lived nearly one hundred years later. The haftarah explains that Jehoida established a covenant between the Lord and the king and the king and the people. It then shifts to King Jehoash who, while attempting to repair the Temple, discovers a corrupt priesthood. Jehoash corrects these injustices and restores some type of order. This is the background for the haftarah for Shabbat Shekalim. Jehoash ruled from 836–798 B.C.E.

Shabbat Shekalim

The final haftarah excerpted from the books of Kings is read on the Second day Passover (2 Kings 23:1–9, 21–25). It relates how King Josiah, after discovering an ancient scroll in the Temple, enacted a series of reforms which transformed the country.

■　■　■

This is the beginning of the fourth nexus point and will be discussed after we summarize the eighth century.

34

The Eighth Century
The Circumstances Leading to the Destruction of the Northern Kingdom
Amos, Hosea, Jonah, Micah, Malachi, and Joel

The eighth century was the most prosperous period in the history of the Northern Kingdom. It is also referred to as *the Persian period*. As a result of close commercial and economic ties with Judah, the weakening of the Aram-Damascus coalition, and the expansion into Bashan and Jauran (the wheat granaries of Israel), a firm economic and agricultural basis that had long been lacking was restored. Jeroboam 2nd (784–748 B.C.E.) expanded the Northern Kingdom and gained control of Syria in the north and as far south as the Dead Sea. For the first time since Solomon's death, the main trade routes joining Mesopotamia and Anatolia with Egypt were controlled by Israel.

It was also the time when a man named Jonah prophesied **Jonah** in front of Jeroboam 2nd, the king of Israel. This is allegedly the same Jonah whose story is read on Yom Kippur. The chief source of social conditions during the reign of Jeroboam 2nd was another prophet named Amos, from the **Amos** village of Tekoah.

Amos was a new type of prophet. He and his contemporaries were not associated with the prophetic guild nor were they attached to a king. Four similar **Hosea, Micah,** prophets were Hosea, Micah, Isaiah, and Joel. Sixteen **Isaiah, Joel** passages were selected from the book of Isaiah by the rabbis in post–Bar Kokbah times to serve as haftarot. Other Isaiah haftarot were written much later and focused on the circumstances leading up to the destruction of the Temple by the Babylonians. The number of haftarot that were selected from the book of Isaiah will be addressed in two separate sections.

Haftarot from Amos and Hosea

Va-yetze	Hosea 12:13–14:10 (Ashkenazi)
	Hosea 11:7–12:2 (Sephardi)
Va-yishlah	Hosea 11:7–12:12 (Ashkenazi)
	Hosea 11:7–12:2 (Sephardi)
Va-yeshev	Amos 2:6–3
Kedoshim (Aharei Mot-Kedoshim)	
	Amos 9:7–15 (Ashkenazi)
Be-midbar	Hosea 2:1-22

This is how it occurred: a farmer living in the hills of Tekoah, sixteen miles south of Jerusalem (indeed he lived in Judah), began to prophesy, or shall we say publicly criticize the king of Israel and the behaviors of the nobility in the Northern Kingdom. Amos criticized their unfair business practices and the over-indulgent excesses being practiced by the priests and royalty in the north. He even went so far as to publicly predict that the king of Israel would die by the sword and the people of Israel would be exiled.

Amos added a new dimension to prophecy. Rather than align himself with a king and his court and concern himself with prophesying about the future of a nation, he disclaimed any allegiance to the prophetic guild and declared, *"I was no prophet, neither was I the son of a prophet; but I was a herdsman and a gatherer of fruit."*

Amos was concerned with the way people of wealth and stature behaved towards others. He believed this was the supreme criteria for judging people. Amos was the first of what we refer to as the literary prophets, and Isaiah followed in his footsteps.

Va-yeshev Amos appeared sometime between twenty and forty years before the Assyrians destroyed the Northern Kingdom. It is within this context that the haftarah Va-yeshev takes place.

Kedoshim The Ashkenazic haftarah for parshat Kedoshim is an excerpt from the last chapter in the book of Amos. In this excerpt, Amos rejects the views of the prophets who linked their prophecies to national destinies or to being "chosen." He makes it extremely clear that God will judge everyone on the basis of their behavior, and "chosenness" cannot trump moral behavior.

While Amos dwelt in Judah and prophesied against the Northern Kingdom, his spiritual successor Hosea lived in the Northern Kingdom and reinterpreted the prophecies he received in a new light.

Hosea

Jeroboam 2nd died in 748 B.C.E. His death marked the beginning of the decline of the Kingdom of Israel. His son, Zachariah, and the remainder of his family, was murdered six months following his ascension to the throne. The next king held the throne for one month before he was murdered. This political instability had economic consequences and the status and prosperity of the country weakened.

The prophecies of Hosea ben Beeri reflect the turmoil of this period. At the same time that the Northern Kingdom was beginning to disintegrate, the political balance of power in the ancient Near East underwent a radical change. Tiglath-Pileser 3rd ascended the throne in 745 B.C.E. and transformed Assyria into a world empire that conquered and cruelly ruled the ancient Near East for the next century.

Hosea ben Beeri

745 B.C.E.

The haftarot selected for parshat Va-yetze, Va-yishlah, and Ba-midbar are set in this period and reflect Hosea's predictions that *Ephraim* (also referred to as Israel and Samaria) would be destroyed. He prophesied that punishment for Israel's transgressions was inevitable and could only be averted if the people repented and returned to the old ways. Hosea understood the current national crisis in a new light. He described the relationship between God and Israel (the Northern Kingdom) as a marriage where the wife had strayed and become involved with other men. Like any husband, God is torn between two feelings. On one hand he is motivated to demonstrate Divine Love towards Israel and will take her back once she reforms, but at the same time, like most men, he feels spurned and wants to punish his estranged lover for her transgressions. Hosea, like his predecessor Elijah, continues to encourage Israel to cease from worshiping Baal and participating in other Canaanite religious practices.

Va-yetze
Va-yishlah
Ba-midbar

The haftarah assigned to parshat Toldot was extracted from
the book of Malachi, where the tension between Jacob and
Esau is mirrored in the haftarah by the separation of the
Northern Kingdom from Judah. Micah prophesied during
the reigns of the Judean monarchs (Jotham, Ahaz, and
Hezekiah), which places his ministry sometime between
758 and 698 B.C.E. Based on some of his statements one can
posit that he prophesied after the fall of Samaria (Northern
Kingdom in 722 B.C.E.) and during the siege of Jerusalem in
701 B.C.E. Micah was a Judean prophet anchored in the
literary tradition of his contemporaries, Amos, Hosea, and
Isaiah. Like Amos and Hosea, he is critical of excess wealth
and immoral behaviors.

*The Siege of Jerusalem! Never heard of it. No wonder these
haftarot are so challenging! But that is Isaiah's story and it is
the subject of the next chapter.*

The death of Jeroboam in 748 B.C.E. marked the beginning
of the decline of the Northern Kingdom. Ten years later a
similar process began in the south and the political balance
of power in the ancient Near East was radically changed as
a result of Tiglath-Pileser 3rd becoming the king of Assyria.
It is the year 745 B.C.E. Today the geographic area of what
was once Assyria is today known as Iraq. Within three years,
Tiglath-Pileser's armies conquered northern and central
Syria with the intention of penetrating as far south as Egypt.

In response to this incursion, alliances were formed
between what remained of Syria (Damascus), the Northern
Kingdom, and Judah. Egypt promised aid and support,
depending upon Assyria's strengths or current weakness.
Judah (Jerusalem) was politically and economically
floundering. Edom had revolted against Judah in 738 B.C.E.
and Judah lost all of its territories beyond the Jordan. At
the same time the city-states of Ashdod and Beth-Shemesh
succeeded in establishing themselves as independent
nations. King Ahaz (King of Judah), fearing conquest from
either Egypt or Israel, reached out to Tiglath-Pileser and
requested support. In return for that support, Judah became
one of Assyria's satraps. This is part of the story of Isaiah.

Tiglath-Pileser invaded the Northern Kingdom in 733–732
B.C.E. and annexed Galilee. He renamed the area *Magiddu*

and made the city of *Meggido* its capital. This left the Kingdom of Israel with little more than the city of Shomrom (Samaria) — that is to say, a little more than a small city surrounded by the hills of Ephraim.

Fate intervened (but was it truly fate?) for a brief period and Tiglath-Pileser died. A decade later a new ruler, Sargon 2nd, seized power. Bottom line: alliances were formed and reformed but nothing could stop the Assyrian advance. In 722 B.C.E., what remained of the Northern Kingdom was conquered and Samaria was resettled with colonists deported from other parts of the Assyrian Empire. At first, the new peoples still worshipped their own gods, but in the course of time, they intermingled with the remaining inhabitants of Samaria. As a result of the Persian conquest of Samaria (Northern Kingdom), a new ethnic religious entity developed. In time these people came to be known as Samaritans.   **Samaritans**

Little information has been preserved about the ten tribes exiled to Assyria. Some people were settled in the vicinity of Gozan on the Habor River. Others were settled in Media.

Within this context, the haftarot for Balak and Hukkat Balak   **Balak and**
were selected from Micah. He prophesied against the   **Hukkat Balak**
leaders in Jerusalem and the Temple and challenged a   **Micah**
corrupt priesthood to change their ways and to honor God
or have *their blessings cursed and their offerings heaved in
their faces.* This occurs either just before the destruction of
the Northern Kingdom (722 B.C.E.) or just prior to the
acquisition of Jerusalem in 701 B.C.E. Micah was a
contemporary of Isaiah. The haftarah for Shabbat Shuvah   **Shabbat Shuvah**
for Asheknazim is a combination of selections from the
prophets Hosea and Joel. Little is known about Joel,   **Hosea**
although the language employed links him to this period   **Joel**
and makes him a contemporary of Hosea and Micah.   **Micah**

■ ■ ■

*The prophet who provides us with the most insight into this
period was the prophet Isaiah. The next chapter is devoted to
him.*

39

Isaiah

First period

In 745 B.C.E. Jeroboam 2nd, the king of the Northern Kingdom, died. At that time Israel was the strongest nation in that part of the ancient world. Under his rule he expanded his kingdom almost to the same size it had been in the days of Solomon. Accompanying this military expansion was a period of great economic prosperity. Three years after Jeroboam's death Isaiah appeared and directed his messages primarily towards Judah.

This was also the time of Amos and Hosea, who unsuccessfully attempted to change the direction of the Northern Kingdom.

Nineteen haftarot were excerpted from Isaiah's book. They can be divided into three different periods. While historians assert that the book of Isaiah had as many as five different authors, for our purposes Isaiah will be divided into three distinct groupings.

The first grouping focuses on the circumstances leading up to the destruction and loss of Israel to the Assyrians (Persians).This grouping focuses on the man who we assume was Isaiah. His career took place in the latter half of the 8th century. He interacted with and influenced four Judean kings: Uzziah (769–733 B.C.E.), Jotham (758–743 B.C.E.), who served as Uzziah's regent as a result of his leprosy, Ahaz (743–727 B.C.E.) and his son Hezekiah (727–698 B.C.E.).

Haftarot in the order of the weekly Torah portions

Bereshit	Isaiah 42:5–43:10
Noah	Isaiah 54:1–55:5
Lekh Lekha	Isaiah 40:27–41:16
Shemot	Isaiah 27:6–28:15, 29:22–23
Yitro	Isaiah 6:1–7:6, 9:5–6
Va-yikra	Isaiah 43:21–44:23
Devarim (Shabbat Hazon)	Isaiah 1:1–27

Va-ethannan (Nahamu)	Isaiah 40:1–26
Ekev	Isaiah 49:14–51:3
Re'eh	Isaiah 54:11–55:5
Shofetim	Isaiah 51:12–52:12
Ki Tetze	Isaiah 54:1–10
Ki Tavo	Isaiah 60:1–22
Nitzvaim	Isaiah 61:10–63:9
Shabbat Rosh Hodesh	Isaiah 66:1–24
Yom Kippur morning	Isaiah 57:14–58:14
Tisha b'Av afternoon	Isaiah 55:6–56:8
Fast day afternoons	(same as above)
Eighth day of Passover	Isaiah 10:32–126

Haftarot attributed to Isaiah in the 8th century.
Isaiah Chapters 1-39

Shemot	Isaiah 27:6–28:15, 29:22–23
Yitro	Isaiah 6:1–7:6, 9:5–6
Devarim (Shabbat Hazon)	Isaiah 1:1–27
Eighth day of Passover	Isaiah 10:32–12:6

Context
The Assyrians were committed to the tremendous task of conquering both Babylonia and Syria. At that time, most of the ancient world was composed of small city-states. The Assyrians plundered the cities and deported significant portions of their populations. They repopulated them with people who were pro-Assyrian in hopes that the populations would eventually blend together and not seek to rebel. In an effort to respond to the Assyrian incursions, Syria and Israel (Damascus and Samaria), and Ashkelon and Gaza, sought an alliance with Judah. Ahaz, the king of Judah, refused to enter into this coalition and as a consequence found himself threatened by the coalition and Jerusalem was besieged. At the same time the Edomites and Phillistines, Judah's southern provinces, took advantage of Judah's political weakness and broke away, leaving Ahaz and the Jerusalemites in a state of panic.

His heart and the heart of his people shook as the trees of the forest shake before the wind. (Isaiah 7:2)

It appeared the only way Ahaz could save his people was to reach out and request aid from the Assyrians. Isaiah counseled differently. Ahaz disagreed. He surrendered Judah's independence to Assyria. Within three years, Assyria conquered the entire Galilee, Gilead, Ashkelon, Gaza, and **732 B.C.E.** Damascus all the way to the Egyptian border. By 732 B.C.E. all that remained of the Northern Kingdom was Samaria. **Yitro** This is the backdrop of Isaiah's message for the haftarah Yitro.

But in actuality this haftarah adds additional dimensions to our understanding. Chapter 9 prophesies the birth of King Hezekiah, the great king, who would rule for forty years. The prophecy proclaiming his birth is one of the key prophecies used by the early church fathers as a biblical proof text to foretell the birth of Jesus. It also formed the basis for Handel's great religious work "The Messiah." On the verge of destruction, Isaiah prophesied that a king would be born who would lead Judah into a more prosperous time.

Shabbat Hazon Sometime after the destruction of the 2nd Temple the rabbis selected Isaiah 1:1–27 to be the haftarah for Shabbat Hazon, the Sabbath prior to the 9th of Av. This haftarah is composed of a series of rebukes against those who were overly proud and ritually and ethically corrupt. It begins explaining that Isaiah prophesied during the rule of four kings, over a period leading up to and following the destruction of the Northern Kingdom. It is part of a series of haftarot directed against both kingdoms. Living in the aftermath of the 2nd Temple's destruction, the rabbis must have understood these rebukes to be the dire consequences of unheeded warnings softened only by Isaiah's closing statement,

> I will restore your magistrates of old, and your counselors of yore. After that you shall be called City of Righteousness, Faithful City. Zion shall be saved in judgment; Her repentant ones, in the retribution. (Isaiah 1:26-27)

While Ahaz, in order to preserve his people, chose to ally with Assyria, Isaiah disagreed. He counseled Ahaz to trust in the Lord and promote more ethical behaviors.

42

Shemot (Ashkenazim)
The haftarah for Shemot is directed at both kingdoms **Shemot**
alternating between threats of destruction and promises of
hope. Paralleling the birth of Moses and the liberation from
Egypt, the haftarah suggests a future time of national
unification if the people of what was once one nation and
then became two nations were capable of comprehending
and modifying their respective behaviors into ethical ones.

The Assyrian king arrived near Jerusalem (Nob) to attack,
but God promised to defeat the mortal king and his army
and to reestablish the Davidic line. This is the context for **Eighth day of**
the haftarah for the eighth day of Passover. **Passover**

Isaiah ministered to four kings of Judah. He was alive when
the Northern Kingdom vanished. He predicted the
subjugation of Judah to Babylon and cautioned Hezekiah
to beware of entangling alliances. In order to fortify
Jerusalem, Hezekiah built a tunnel which brought water
underneath the hill of Jerusalem to a pool within its walls.

> Behold the days are coming, when all that is in your
> house, and that which our fathers have stored up to
> this day, shall be carried to Babylon. Some of your
> own sons will be eunuchs in the palace of the King
> of Babylon. (Isaiah 39:5-7)

Isaiah preached that God could be likened to a father who
had been abandoned by his children. He is angry and he is
remorseful. He desires to be one with his people but that
will only occur if his people believe in Him, act justly, and
are wary of political alliances.

43

NEXUS 4
THE DESTRUCTION OF THE FIRST TEMPLE

••

Introduction

This chapter and the one that follows attempt to explain the circumstances leading up to the destruction of the First Temple and Jerusalem. It is followed by a section that summarizes the process leading up to the rebuilding of the Temple and explains how the prophetic period came to a close approximately two hundred years later, depending upon where one begins.

These chapters introduce us to Ezekiel, Jeremiah, Haggai, Zechariah, Malachi, Gedaliah, and Ezra. Haggai, Zechariah, and Malachi were the last Prophets in our tradition. Gedaliah and Ezra, while their names are possibly not household names, played an important part in the development of Jewish life as we know it today.

If you just opened this material in order to learn about a specific haftarah and skipped what preceded it, you need to understand that what we today call Israel and what the Bible refers to as *Judah* was a little province caught between two warring empires, Egypt and Babylon. From the period following 721 B.C.E. (remember we are counting downwards) when the Northern Kingdom was conquered by the Assyrians, what we refer to as *Judah* (Jerusalem) was under constant threat of being conquered by one country or another. In most instances when the Bible refers to the kings of Judah, you need to understand that with rare exception they were not true kings. They were vassals.

Enter Josiah: A Small Fish in a Big Pond

Haftarot

2nd day of Passover	2 Kings 23:1–19, 21–25
Va-era	Ezekiel 28:25–29:21
Tzav	Jeremiah 7:21–8:3, 9:22–23
Aharei Mot	Ezekiel 22:1–19

Judah experienced a brief period of independence during the rule of King Josiah. Josiah was a major player and it's worth reading the chapters devoted to him in the 2nd book of Kings. He changed the way the nation functioned. His reforms were undertaken between 628–609 B.C.E. and his reign can be considered as important as those of David and Solomon. The 2nd book of Kings, chapters 22–23, dates this event to be 621 B.C.E. The book of Chronicles, included in our Bible, but which very few of us have ever read, dates it to be 628 B.C.E. The 2nd book of Chronicles describes his activities in fuller detail. Both texts tell a story of the discovery of a scroll in the Temple in Jerusalem. After reading it, Josiah radically transforms his government and his nation.

In ancient times the "discovery of a scroll" could have referred to the publishing of a book. Most scholars believe the scroll was Deuteronomy chapters 12–25, or what we today call parshat *Re'eh, Shof'tim and Ki Tetze*i. This is how the "book" was discovered.

When Josiah became king, he decided that the Temple which hadn't been maintained for centuries, was in need of repair. The roof was leaking, the furniture hadn't been changed for centuries, and the drapes — oh my, the drapes! During the course of repairs, and this was without a building fund, a Book of Law was discovered.

This event kicked off a national religious awakening ending in a major Passover celebration. An impressive ceremony of rededication of the covenant was organized and like

Moses and Joshua before him, the words of the Torah and the reaffirmation of the covenant took place.

While this was occurring Assyria was forced to recall its troops to fend off other incursions, and Josiah took advantage of their withdrawal and successfully liberated Samaria (the Northern Kingdom) without bloodshed. After decades of continued vassalage, Judah, for a brief period, became independent.

The story of the Passover celebration is found in 2 Kings 23:1–9, 21–25, and is the haftarah which is read on the second day of Passover.

What did Josiah do?

Josiah eliminated the foreign cultic practices which his grandfather Manasseh (2 Kings 22–3) had permitted. He removed the chariots of the sun and vessels of Baal and the *asherot*, which were ancient cultic symbols originating in Phoenicia (2 Kings 23:4, 11). He also eliminated the high places (*bamot*) throughout the country. *Bamot* were high places dedicated to the worshipping of other gods. This effort culminated in the destruction of the venerated center at Bethel.

Bethel

In addition, he restructured the priesthood and established Jerusalem as the only place sacrifices could be offered. He brought the priests who had been administering and offering sacrifices at the high places and at other places of worship in Judah to Jerusalem. He considered them to be priests but not equals. These non-Kohen priests were forbidden from officiating at offerings in the Temple. Yes, sadly, this is where you Levites most likely came from. Finally, he reaffirmed David's bloodline as the only legitimate rulers of Israel.

> And it came to pass; when the King heard the words of the book of the Law he rent his clothes. He commanded Hilkiah, the priest and Ahikam, the son of Shaphan and Achbor, the son of Michiah and Shaphan the scribe, and Asahiah, a servant of the King saying, Go enquire of the Lord for me, and for all the people of Judah, concerning the

words of this book that has been found; for great is
the wrath of the Lord that is kindled against us,
because our fathers did not heed the words of this
book. (2 Kings 22:11-13)

During the final years of his reign the Chaldeans and the
Medes gradually expanded their influence over most of Iraq.
In 614 B.C.E. the Medes attacked and destroyed Ninevah.
(Do you remember the story of Jonah?) Yes, Ninevah was
finally destroyed. Josiah died in 609 B.C.E. while attempting
to halt the Egyptian army near Megiddo. Megiddo was a
key spot on the route between Egypt and the north.

The Temple was destroyed twenty-five years later in 586
B.C.E. The period between 614–605 B.C.E. was most likely
the time when Habakkuk, an extremely minor prophet, **Second day of**
lived. He had a vision of Jerusalem's destruction and only **Shavout:**
one haftarah is accorded to him. It is read on the second **Habakkuk**
day of Shavout: Habakkuk 3:1-19. **3:1–19**

*If Josiah knew how his children and grandchildren behaved,
he wouldn't be happy.*

Josiah was succeeded by his son Jehoahaz, and Judah
became a province of Egypt. The new Pharaoh removed
him as king, exiled him to Egypt appointing his elder
brother Eliakim, whom he renamed and called *Jehoiakim*
to be his successor. Jehoiakim has the title *king* but let's
face it, the word *governor* would be more appropriate.

Judah remained an Egyptian territory for five years
(609–604 B.C.E.), before it was once again acquired by
Babylon. The throne of Judah changed hands four times
within the next twenty years.

Jehoiakim, caught between Egypt and Babylon, played a
complicated double game. He cultivated Egypt and at the
same time gave lip service to Babylon. Seeking proof of
Babylonian weakness in 601–600 B.C.E., he withheld tribute
and declared a rebellion. Egypt promised support but was
unfortunately defeated in battle by the Babylonians. In
response to the Egyptian loss, Jeremiah proclaimed a fast **Jeremiah**

and announced that Nebuchadnezzar, the king of Babylon, was an instrument of God's divine anger.

Nebuchadnezzar, the king of Babylon, was not pleased with Jehoiakim's resistance. It took three years for him to organize and invade Judah. On the eve of conquest Jehoiakim died, leaving his eighteen-year-old son in charge with the Babylonian army approaching Jerusalem. Wisely, he surrendered. Nebuchadnezzar appointed Jehoiakim's nephew *Mattanaih* to succeed him and changed his name to *Zedekiah*. It is 604 B.C.E.; the Temple was destroyed eighteen years later.

Jeremiah
Ezekiel
The Prophets who lived during the period leading up to the Temple's destruction were Jeremiah and Ezekiel. Jeremiah prophesied in Judah from the 13th year of Josiah (627 B.C.E.) to the 11th year of Zedekiah (586 B.C.E.). I know we haven't discussed Zedekiah, but don't worry, we will.

Jeremiah lived through a period of national independence at a time when the control of Judah was transferred to Egypt and then back to Babylon. He also lived through the period of the first and second forced exiles. It was during the second exile that the Temple, Jerusalem, and the province of Judah were destroyed. Did I say first and second exiles? Whoops!

The initial dispersion, or as some say, exile, took place in 597 B.C.E., thirteen years before the Temple's destruction. At that time the so-called "intelligentsia," people of wealth, priests, royalty, artists, and craftspeople, were uprooted and forcibly deported to Babylon. The deportation was a Babylonian punishment for Jehoiakim's behavior. The **Ezekiel** prophet Ezekiel was part of this initial deportation. Between eight and ten thousand people were deported in 597 B.C.E.

The second deportation (exile) occurred thirteen years later. At that time, the Temple and Jerusalem had already been **Jeremiah** conquered and destroyed. Some people, including Jeremiah, fled south to Egypt. Nebuchadnezzar, the Babylonian king, allowed the poor to remain. Jeremiah continued to issue his prophecies of rebukes from Egypt until 583 B.C.E.

And in the fifth month on the seventh day of the
month, which is the 19th year of King
Nebuchadnezar, King of Babylon, Nebuzaradan,
(Captain of the guard), came to Jerusalem. He burnt
the house of the Lord, and the King's house, and all
the house of Jerusalem, every great man's house he
burnt with fire. And the Chaldean army that was
with him broke down the walls of Jerusalem. And
Nebuzarad, the Captain of the Guard carried away
all the rest of the people that remained in the city
including the spoils of the city and the Temple
vessels. And Nebuzarad left the poor. (2 Kings 25:8)

To a great extent Ezekiel's and Jeremiah's prophecies reflect
the politics of this tempestuous period. This is the setting **Va-era**
for haftarot Va-era and Tzav. **Tzav**

Va-era
Ezekiel 28:25–29:21
This haftarah is a prophecy directed against Egypt, warning
Judah not to ally with them against Babylon. This prophecy
was, of course, ignored and resulted in the Temple's
destruction. This haftarah was probably written during the
last days of the Temple.

Tzav
Jeremiah 7:21–8:3, 9:22–23
Tzav warns of a coming judgment against the Temple and
the nation if they don't change their ways. This was also
written prior to the Temple's destruction, most likely after
the death of Josiah. Makes sense, doesn't it?

The prophecies of Jeremiah and Ezekiel were not always
prophecies of doom and gloom. Jeremiah's early prophecies
encouraged the kings of Judah to avoid political alliances
and to trust in the Lord. His prophecies or political
warnings were consistently ignored. Once he offended the
king, and in order to save his life was forced to flee to Egypt.
Over time, as the situation in Judah deteriorated, his
prophecies became stronger and warned of imminent
destruction if our people did not change their ways.

After the Temple's destruction his prophecies changed from those of doom and gloom to those which offered comfort and rebirth. The book of Lamentations, which is chanted on the 9th of Av (Tisha b'Av), was allegedly written by Jeremiah.

597 B.C.E. If you recall, Ezekiel was exiled to Babylon along with 8,000 to 10,000 other exiles in the year 597 B.C.E. This occurred during King Jehoiakim's brief reign, who along with his court was also deported. Ezekiel and his compatriots were settled in Tel Abib, "Mound of the Flood," a city located on the River Chebar, a tributary canal of the Euphrates, which was southeast of Babylon.

593 B.C.E. He began to prophesy in 593 B.C.E. His initial prophecies were condemnations and prophecies of doom for the Judeans remaining in Judah and Jerusalem. These prophecies are found in the first twenty-four chapters of his book. They stopped, or shall we say changed, two years before the final destruction in 588.

Why?

It could be that after trying to challenge the people of Judah to repent for five years, he realized it wasn't going to happen. The situation in Jerusalem worsened day by day.

Or, perhaps he just became frustrated! After all, why should the people in Jerusalem believe him? It is true that he, like Jeremiah, was a priest, and as a priest had a vested interest in the Temple and probably still had some gravitas; but then again, who would have known him in Jerusalem after eighteen years of exile?

While he was living in Jerusalem, before he began to prophesy, he could have been just another priest of aristocratic lineage. And then, imagine, he gets transported nearly 500 miles to the north and all of a sudden becomes a prophet! An expatriate prophet? Who would listen to him!

I am guessing that it took at least three months for the news of Jerusalem's destruction to travel nearly six hundred miles as the crow flies and nearly twice that distance by the caravan routes before Ezekiel learned that Jerusalem had been destroyed. The news of the destruction could have been the reason for his prophecies changing. All of a sudden prophecies of doom were transformed to prophecies that offered spiritual consolation and predicted national reunification and cultic restoration. A vision of a restored 3rd Temple emerged and was dated at 573 B.C.E., two years before his last prophecy in 571 B.C.E. What could be more comforting? These prophecies are found in Ezekiel chapters 33–39 and 40–48.

Gedaliah
Jehoiakim
Zedekiah

It is also likely that Ezekiel and Jeremiah knew or knew of Gedaliah, Jehoiakim, and Zedekiah. The haftarah for Aharei Mot (Ezekiel 22:1–19) was written some years before the Temple's destruction.

Aharei Mot
(Ezekiel
22:1–19)

••

Destruction and the End of Autonomy
The Last Picture Show, or Was It?

In order to be appointed as governor, Zedekiah, the last king (pardon me, governor) of Judah and the grandnephew of the great King Josiah, was forced to swear an oath of fealty to Babylon.

This didn't exactly endear him to a lot of people who lived in Judah and in Babylon. Both groups must have perceived him as a Babylonian puppet. Remember, this was a time when a significant portion of the Judean population had recently been exiled to Bablyon, and the exiled court was actually living in Babylon. It is logical to assume that people in Judah continued to communicate with their exiled friends and family members.

Egypt continued to vie for power and sought to create a buffer zone against a future Babylonian invasion. The Egyptian monarch Pharoah Psammetichus 2 convinced Zedekiah (the last Judean king) to revolt against Babylon and promised military support. The support lasted for one battle where the Egyptian army fought the Babylonians to a standstill, but for reasons not to be explained, immediately following that battle, military support ceased. Imagine how

Nebuchadnezzar must have felt when he learned that his vassal Zedekiah had rebelled against him. Not pleased.

Zedekiah should have studied Isaiah. He might have learned something.

> When the army of the Chaldeans (Babylonians) raised the siege of Jerusalem on account of the army of Pharaoh. (Jeremiah 37:11)

Bo This is the context for the haftarah for parshat Bo. The haftarah also describes an incident that took place a few decades earlier just after the death of King Josiah. Josiah, if you recall, was killed fighting the Egyptians in 609 B.C.E. His efforts delayed Egypt's attack long enough for the Babylonians to rally their armies and prevent an Egyptian victory. Neco, the Pharaoh, attempted to strengthen his position by removing Josiah's son, Jehoahaz, from the throne and replaced him with his pro-Egyptian brother Jehoiakim. But the Egyptians were turned back. Jeremiah warned the people not to form alliances with Egypt.

Our ancestors used this chapter, this prophecy, to warn the people living twenty- two years later to also refrain from forming alliances with Egypt.

> Then King Zedekiah sent for Jeremiah and asked secretly in his palace, "Is there any word from the Lord?" "There is!" Jeremiah answered, "You will be delivered into the hands of the king of Babylon." (Jeremiah 37:17)

As soon as Nebuchadnezzar learned of the alliance and the revolt, he responded aggressively and after a brief period conquered Jerusalem.

Mishpatim (Jeremiah 34:8–22, 33:25–26) The haftarah for parshat Mishpatim (Jeremiah 34:8–22, 33:25–26) provides another view of the final siege of Jerusalem. It states that on the eve of Jerusalem's destruction, Jeremiah promises the people of Judah that God will not forsake them. This theme is further developed in parshat **Behar (Jeremiah 32:6–7)** Behar (Jeremiah 32:6–7) when at the time of the destruction, God symbolically promises Jerusalem's restoration.

Nebuchadnezzar punished Zedekiah and his family according to the custom and laws of his country. Zedekiah's family was killed in his presence and he was blinded and sent to Babylon in chains. Oh, did I forget to mention the Temple was destroyed and thousands of additional people were exiled!

> They slaughtered Zedekiah's sons before his eyes; then Zedekiah's eyes were put out. He was chained in bronze fetters and brought to Babylon. (2 Kings 25:7-8)

Post-Destruction

Jerusalem was destroyed but Nebuchadnezzar still required a governor. He appointed Gedaliah and began to call what used to be referred to as "Judah" the "Yehud" province.

> King Nebuchadnezzar put Gedaliah, son of Ahikam in charge of the people who he left in the land of Judah. (2 Kings 25:22)

With Jerusalem in ruins the city of Mizpah became the new **Mizpah** provincial capital. Gedaliah took his position seriously and attempted to revitalize and normalize Jewish life. His first reform was to legalize the status of the land by recognizing the people who were tilling it as owners. In that way the poorest of the land, those who were not exiled, were able to gain possession.

The fate of the Israelites and other peoples exiled to Assyria had taught him that exiled people never return to their native lands. It is likely that those who remained in Judah (Yehud) considered themselves to be the survivors of the Israelite people. This view was strongly opposed by the prophet Ezekiel, who envisioned a return.

Gedaliah's efforts at reform and reorganization were cut short by the anti-Babylon faction led by one of the descendants of Zedekiah's family, who were still loyal to the house of Zedekiah (the descendant of King David). They assassinated him and fled with their followers and with Jeremiah to . . . where else but Egypt! This took place

53

around 582 B.C.E., four years after the Temple's destruction. The death of Gedaliah represented the last bastion of Jewish sovereignty, or at least Jewish autonomy. His history and its aftermath are found in Jeremiah 41–45.

Fast of Gedaliah This is the Gedaliah who the rabbis, living after the destruction of the 2nd Temple some 600 plus years later, remembered with honor. In his memory they instituted a fast which takes place the day after Rosh Hashanah, and it is called the Fast of Gedaliah.

The first reference to The Fast of Gedaliah occurs in the book of Zechariah chapters 7-8, where Zechariah refers to four fast days associated with the destruction of Judah, the fast of the 17th of Tammuz, the 9th of Av, the 15th of Av, and the fast of Gedaliah. Even though the prophet Zechariah lived at least fifty years after Gedaliah's death and refers to a fast in his memory, we can't be certain that it had become a national day of mourning during that time. We can assume that by the fourth century C.E. people were observing the Fast of Gedaliah.

Haftarot
The haftarot which reflect the period leading up to the Temple's destruction occur in the following parshiot:

Bo	Jeremiah 6:13–28
	After Egypt's defeat by Nebuchadnezzar
	around 604 B.C.E.
Mishpatim	Jeremiah 34:22, 33:2–26
	Final siege of Jerusalem
Emor	Jeremiah 44:15–31
	Post-destruction
Behar	Jeremiah 32:6–27
	Nebuchadnezzar's armies besieging
	Jerusalem
Pinhas	Jeremiah 1:1–2:3
Mato-Masei	Either Jeremiah 1:1–2:3
	or Jeremiah 2:4–28, 3:4

Pinhas Matot-Masei Remember: Jeremiah lived through the period of the Temple's destruction. The following two haftarot (Pinhas after the 17th of Tammuz and Matot-Masei) were written just prior to the Temple's destruction.

■ ■ ■

Jewish autonomy, for all intents and purposes, ended with the death of Gedaliah. The Temple and Jerusalem were in ruins and our ancestors had been transported to a strange new land, which happened to be the most sophisticated society in the world at that time. How they responded is the subject of the next section. This is the story of second Isaiah.

NEXUS 5

CYRUS AND
CAN WE EVER REALLY GO HOME?

••

The Temple was destroyed in 586 B.C.E. and our ancestors were exiled to the most sophisticated urban environment in the world. Imagine being raised in a small town in Iowa and suddenly being uprooted and transported to live in Manhattan or a close suburb like Teaneck, NJ. Initially it must have been a traumatic heartbreaking experience. On the other hand, living in the capital of the world did have some advantages, and like our grandparents or great-grandparents who fled from Europe and came to a new world, our ancestors began to adjust.

Very little is known about the organization or history of the land of Judah between 596 and 538 B.C.E., but a considerable amount of information about the Judean exiles in Babylon during Nebuchadnezzar's reign can be ascertained from the book of Ezekiel and additional sources.

Within a generation the refugees began to adapt to Babylonian culture. They took Persian names like Mordecai, Esther, and Zerubabel (seed of Babylon), and they replaced the names of the Hebrew months which were numbered months (1st month, 7th month, and so on) with their Babylonian counterparts — e.g., Sivan, Adar, Nisan, etc. They learned to speak the language and integrated themselves into a tolerant Persian society. It took a while, but 50 years later when Cyrus the Great conquered Babylon and became the King of Persia and Media (remember your Purim story), a number of our ancestors had adjusted and had prospered in this new environment.

It is possible that prophecies preached or published by Ezekiel some fifty-plus years earlier offered our ancestors the necessary consolation and helped them adjust to their new lives. It is also possible that the first generation of exiles expected their exile to be temporary. People living in those times believed that they inherited the guilt and the burden of their ancestors. God punished not just the guilty but those who followed them. Like their descendants some six hundred odd years later who lived through the destruction of the Second Temple, our ancestors living in Babylon could have believed that God would return them to the Promised Land once the punishment had ceased.

Perhaps this was why Ezekiel emphasized personal responsibility: *the son shall not bear the iniquity of the father; neither shall the father bear the iniquity of the son* (Ezekiel 18:20). He argued that the generation of Zedekiah was not punished for the sins of the generation of his father Manasseh.

Ezekiel 18:20

He also argued that only repentance could obviate the punishment. Perhaps after the Temple's destruction the people realized that the exile might last for a long time. *Our bones are dried, and our hope is lost* (Ezekiel 37:11). Perhaps that is why we read on the intermediate Shabbat of Passover his response in chapter 37:1–10, which predicted a national rebirth *when the bones are recovered with flesh.*

Intermediate Shabbat of Passover

It is interesting that the feelings of reward and punishment that our ancestors might have experienced in exile, after the first Temple's destruction, were mirrored by the beliefs of our ancestors living in the aftermath of the Second Temple's destruction by the Romans some 600 years later.

Significant changes took place in the religious and cultural perceptions in the exiled community. Idolatry seemed to have disappeared and the community became more insular. One would think that as time progressed and as our ancestors became more assimilated, their beliefs and customs would be modified by the larger culture.

Ezekiel provided them with a religious vision. He encouraged them to remember that exile, just like return, was part of God's plan and that redemption was going to occur at some future time. As a result of hearing this message for approximately fifty years, many of our ancestors could have believed that Cyrus, the man who united the kingdoms of Medes to Persia, was God's instrument of redemption. It is also possible that our ancestors, the thousands of educated people who had been living in Babylon since 597 B.C.E. and who had been integrated into Babylonian society, even encouraged Cyrus to invade Babylon.

··

Cyrus and the Implications of Return

Haftarot

2nd Isaiah or Deutero-Isaiah (written in Babylonia post–586 B.C.E.). Chapters 40–55.

Bereshit	Isaiah 42:5–43:10
Noah	Isaiah 54:1–37
Lekh Lekha	Isaiah 40:27–41:16
Vayikra	Isaiah 43:21–44:23

Va-ethannan (Shabbat Nahamu, the Sabbath of Consolation)
	Isaiah 40:1–26
Ekev	Isaiah 49:14–51:3
Re'eh	Isaiah 54:11–55:5
Shofetim	Isaiah 51:12–2:12
Ki Tetze	Isaiah 54:1–10

3rd Isaiah or Trito-Isaiah (written in Palestine post–439 B.C.E.). Chapters 56–66.

Ki Tavo	Isaiah 60:1–22
Nitzvaim and Nitzavim-Va'yelekh	Isaiah 60:1–63:9
Shabbat Rosh Hodesh	Isaiah 66:1–24
Yom Kippur morning	Isaiah 57:14–58:14
Tisha b'Av afternoon	Isaiah 55:6–56:8

Consider that fourteen haftarot were selected by the rabbis, nine of which focus on the circumstances just prior to or immediately after Cyrus became the ruler of Babylon in 539 B.C.E. The final five belong to another prophet, also called Isaiah, who could have lived in Jerusalem at the end of the sixth century and was a contemporary of two of the last three prophets, Haggai and Zechariah. Some scholars actually claim he lived and wrote much later — that is to say, around the time of Ezra and Nehemia 460 B.C.E.

What does matter was that the rabbis selected a significant number of passages for haftarot from the time after the destruction of the first Temple and around the time that the second one was authorized and perhaps even in the process of being constructed.

One of Cyrus' first acts after becoming emperor was to issue an edict permitting the Judeans to return to their homeland and to renew their ancestral practices.

The first wave of returnees was led by Sheshbazzar, the prince of Judah (Ezra 1:8), who was possibly the son of Jehoiakim. Ezra informs us that he received the Temple vessels from the Persian treasurer. It is possible that Sheshbazzar was appointed governor of Judah. His place was eventually assumed by Zerubabel son of Shealtiel, the grandson of Jehoiakim. This took place in the year 539 B.C.E.

539 B.C.E.

The order of events leading up to the completion of the construction of the Second Temple, as well as the leadership of the time, is still open to debate. According to Ezra, Jeshua the Priest and Zerubabel led the returnees. Their first action was to erect an altar and reinstitute sacrifice.

Conflicts developed between the returnees and the "people of the land" in the earliest stages of the Temple's reconstruction. The "people of the land," who were living in or near Jerusalem when the first returnees arrived, saw themselves as equal members of the Jewish people. This group requested to be allowed to participate in the Temple's restoration. Zerubabel did not respond kindly. *"You have nothing to do with us to build a house to God; we will build it to the Lord God of Israel as King Cyrus commanded us"* (Ezra 4:3).

The lack of support and the tensions that arose between these two groups as well as the tensions which developed between the local leaders of other cities (who saw the rebuilding as a threat to their power and autonomy) and Zerubabel's followers, hindered the reconstruction. Once the altar had been constructed, work began on the Temple foundations. We have record that this occurred right away. For some reason, possibly because of the way Zerubabel treated the "people of the land," who could have been descendants of the original settlers, the Temple's reconstruction ground to a standstill.

When the news of the rebuilding reached the governor of Trans-Euphrates, he challenged the right of the returnees to build the Temple and reported this to Darius (Ezra 5:3–17). Since the edict had been proclaimed verbally and the written text, the official records, were not in Jerusalem, our ancestors were not able to initially prove they were actually operating with the emperor's permission. Darius, the son of Cyrus, ordered a search in the royal archives and the original documents were eventually discovered. The decree was deemed valid and instructions were issued to complete the Temple and fund the expenses from the satrap's treasury. Darius added an additional requirement that a sacrifice be offered for the welfare of the king and his sons in the completed Temple. This became a regularly practiced custom in the Second Temple period and continued until the Great Revolt against the Romans in 68 C.E. and according to Neil Gillman is the origin of the prayer **520 B.C.E.** for our country. It is the year 520 B.C.E.

In the period between the rise of Cyrus and the ministries of Haggai and Zechariah, someone who we refer to as Isaiah began to prophesy. When he began his ministry he found the people of the Lord believed that God was "hiding his face" and their cause was hopeless. This is the focus of the **Lekh Lekha** haftarah for Lekh Lekha. *"Why do you say, O Jacob, and speak that their case was hopeless: Why do you say, O Jacob* **Isaiah 40:27** *my way is hid from the Lord"* (Isaiah 40:27).

Isaiah counseled against these feelings of despair and instead offered comfort and encouragement. He preached to the exiles that a time of new hope and new spirit would arrive. It could be that this haftarah was written shortly before or after Cyrus permitted the resettlement of Jerusalem.

60

Isaiah's prophecies were not confined to offering hope and comfort. He also provided a vision of what redemption meant. Isaiah interpreted Cyrus's conquest of Babylon as a sign that God had fulfilled the first promises and would fulfill "new promises" as well. New promises were equivalent to redemption, the revival of a people, and the return to their homeland. This is the substance of haftarah Ekev and is part of a general theme that pervades the haftarot in Shofetim, Re'eh, Ki Tissa, and Ki Tavo. Is it any wonder that these themes begin the Shabbat prior to the ninth of Av and continue for the following seven weeks!

Ekev
Shofetim
Re'eh
Ki Tissa
Ki Tavo

Haggai and Zechariah, two of the final three prophets

In September 520 B.C.E., prompted by the prophecies of Haggai (Hag 1:2–11, 13–15; 2:2–9), Zerubabel joined Joshua the high priest and through their combined efforts the construction resumed (Ezra 3:8–13). The Temple was finally completed in 515 B.C.E. (Ezra 6:15).

Two of the last three prophets, Haggai and Zechariah, lived during this period and most likely understood the politics of the day to be part of God's plan. Haggai (1:4) tells us that the work on the Temple recommenced in 519 B.C.E. Zechariah's story coincides with the Temple's work stoppage. Twenty-three years after Cyrus permitted the Temple's rebuilding, the work was finally completed.

Haggai
Zechariah

Zechariah is the 11th book of the Minor Prophets, which we refer to as "the 12." Two haftarot are excerpted from Zechariah. One is read during the normal weekly Torah reading and corresponds to the Torah portion Beha'alotecha. That portion is read again on the first Shabbat of Hanukkah. The second excerpt is the haftarah for the first day of Sukkoth. Even though Zechariah and Haggai were contemporaries, the rabbis living after the destruction of the Second Temple did not select a haftarah from Haggai's book. Not that he wasn't important, but for some reason Zechariah's words or deeds trumped Haggai's message.

Beha'alotecha
First Shabbat of Hanukkah
First day of Sukkoth

The book of Zechariah is attributed to Zechariah son of Bershia son of Iddo (Zech 1:1), who began to prophesy, as did Haggai (1:1), during the second year of reign of King Darius 1 (520 B.C.E.). Zechariah is also mentioned in the books of Ezra and Nehemiah. If he was the same Zechariah as Zechariah the son of Bershia the son of Iddo, he was most likely a priest.

Have you noticed how many of our prophets were priests and how many governors of Judea were descended from King David? The third chapter of Zechariah's book focuses on his involvement in the rebuilding of the Temple and his vision for the high priest Joshua.

Zechariah envisions the resumption of the Davidic dynasty under Zerubabel, whom he calls "my servant the branch" (Zechariah 3:8).

> Thus spoke the Lord saying Behold the man whose name is Branch; and he shall grow up out of this place, and he shall build the temple of the Lord: and he shall sit and rule upon his throne; and he shall be a priest upon his throne; and the counsel of peace shall be between them both. (Zech 6:12-13)

515 B.C.E. Zechariah's influence was strongest between 520 and 518 B.C.E. He could have had significant influence helping to recruit support to rebuild the Temple, which according to Ezra 6:5 was completed in 515 B.C.E.

Zechariah and Haggai could have worked together. They most likely knew one another and their ministries overlapped for several months. We can also surmise that Zechariah was involved with the rebuilding of the Temple in more than a prophetic way. Some historians conjecture that Zechariah, the priest, was part of a larger messianic movement that centered around Zerubabel, a descendant of David (6:9-15), because he wished to see the Davidic monarchy returned to power.

Themes of Zechariah Chapters 1–8

Zechariah introduces us to Zerubabel, the grandson of King Jeconiah of Judah, who if you recall, was exiled to

Babylonia in 597 B.C.E. Darius appointed Zerubabel 597 B.C.E.
governor of the province of Yehud (Judah) (Hag 1:1; Ezra
6:15). According to I Chronicles 3:19, Zerubabel's father
was Pedaiah, but other references call him the son of
Shealtiel (both were sons of Jeconiah), Bottom line: he was
Davidic royalty.

Haggai's prophecies indicated that Zerubabel would be the
focus of messianic hopes. He expected the Lord to
overthrow all kingdoms and to elect Zerubabel as his
"servant." He is called "God's chosen" and his "signet ring" Be-ha'alotekha
(Hag 2:21–23). Zechariah's reference to "the Branch" (Zech
3:8) is similarly interpreted to refer to Zerubabel (Haftarah Shabbat
be-ha'alotekha and Shabbat Hanukkah). Hanukkah

It is not known when Zerubabel's activity began or ended.
Some texts state that Zerubabel was the leader of the first
group which returned from the Exile (Ezra 2:2; Neh 7:7)
and that he was involved in building the altar and laying
the Temple foundations in the years 538–537 B.C.E. (Ezra
3:2, 8; 4:2).

Others say he was the first governor of Judah and that the
leader of the first group was Sheshbazzar (Ezra 1:8–11;
5:14, 16). In order to account for the discrepancy, it has
been suggested that Sheshbazzar was the leader in name
only, and that Zerubabel bore the responsibility for all
practical activity. On the other hand, it has been pointed
out that Zechariah credits Zerubabel with laying the
foundations for the Temple, while ignoring the role played
by Sheshbazzar (Zech 4:9).

Haftarot
Be-ha'alotekha, Shabbat Hanukkah
Zechariah 2:14–4:7
Anticipates God's return and the building of the new
Temple. This was probably when Zechariah ended the work
stoppage along with Haggai. Note the reference to
Zerubabel (a descendant of David).

2nd Day of Sukkot
Zechariah 14:1–21
The themes for this haftarah focus on the fulfillment of God's promise and notes that the Temple will be rebuilt and God will right all wrongs.

Let's review

Ezekiel and Jeremiah lived before, during, and after the Temple was destroyed. Haggai and Zechariah were allegedly instrumental in making certain the Temple was rebuilt. Malachi and one of the Isaiahs were the last of our prophets. They lived and prophesied after the Temple had been completed and during the period when the rest of the city was being restored.

The haftarot that were excerpted from Isaiah chapters 56–66 constitute the final phase of the book of Isaiah. These texts most likely correspond to the near end of the prophetic period, the time of Ezra and Nehemia. The Temple had been rebuilt and Isaiah, like Malachi the last of our prophets, is concerned with the nature of priestly conduct. That is the essence of the haftarah for Yom Kippur morning. While Isaiah sought a new beginning, as evinced in the haftarah for Shabbat Rosh Hodesh, he was concerned and critical in the tradition of Amos, who lived hundreds of years earlier, that the priesthood had become corrupt and that their behavior continued to be immoral.

Yom Kippur morning

Shabbat Rosh Hodesh

Haftarot

Ki Tavo	Isaiah 60:1–22
Nitzvaim and Nitzavim-Va'yelekh	Isaiah 60:1–63:9
Shabbat Rosh Hodesh	Isaiah 66:1–24
Yom Kippur morning	Isaiah 57:14–58:14

■ ■ ■

The prophetic period was rapidly drawing to a close. Malachi, the last of the prophets, closes the period some sixty years later. That is the subject of the next and final section.

Malachi and Ezra
The End and the Beginning

Haftarot

Parshat Toldot Malachi 1:2:7
Shabbat HaGadol Malachi 3:4–24

The period between the completion of the Temple (515 B.C.E.) and the arrival of Ezra the Scribe (458 B.C.E.), lasting **458 B.C.E.** more than half a century, is barely documented. We can only surmise what life must have been like in ancient Judah. It seems reasonable to assume that a high priest, the descendant of Zerubabel, administered the Temple and the adjoining areas. This would have been in accordance with Persian practices. We believe that close ties developed between the families of the high priest, leading nobles and officials in Jerusalem, and the leading families in Samaria. The nobility in Samaria accepted Jerusalem and Temple as their religious center and recognized the authority of the high priest in matters of worship and religious leadership. Based upon the text in Zechariah and parts of Isaiah (which were written during this period), one suspects that close relationships between the people living in Samaria and their priesthood existed. It is likely their worldview was universalistic and inclusive.

In 458 B.C.E. Artaxerxes, the king of Persia, granted permission to Ezra the Scribe to lead another wave of returnees to Judah. This was most likely prompted by a need to strengthen the Persian presence with new settlers loyal to the empire.

We don't know a lot about our ancestors living in Babylon, but we do know they had Babylonian or Persian names and they were engaged in agriculture, fishing, and minor government service. We believe that they still felt a link with our homeland and they worshipped in community assemblies and they substituted prayers about sacrifice for sacrifices. Living as Jews in a non-Jewish world, they retained their exclusiveness through worship and what was developing into what we would refer to today as "Jewish law."

In order to maintain their identities *vis-à-vis* the larger Babylonian society they embraced a set of special rules of purity, typical of priests. They only ate certain foods, observed the Sabbath, and celebrated holidays as a group. This sense of exclusiveness was destined to clash with the predominating view among the Jerusalem priesthood and people.

The catalyst for this clash was Ezra the Scribe, Ezra the Priest. Ezra is often associated with a man named Nehemiah. Nehemiah served as a cup-bearer to King Artaxerxes, the king of Persia (445/444 B.C.E.). He successfully overcame the opposition of the Samaritans, Ammonites, Arabs, and Philistines and rebuilt the walls of Jerusalem. He served as Jerusalem's governor for twelve years and assisted Ezra in championing the law of Moses and enforcing the divorce of Jewish men from their non-Jewish wives. A number of discrepancies exist surrounding their dates and some of their accomplishments. For our purpose we are mostly going to focus on Ezra.

Ezra holds a significant place in our religious tradition. A book in the Bible is named in his memory but one could attend synagogue services for one hundred years and never, with the exception of an occasional verse on the High Holidays, hear his name mentioned.

Yehud

After more than one hundred years of living in Babylon, of being urban sophisticates, many of our ancestors chose not to return to Yehud. They probably reasoned, "Life is good in Babylon. Every morning I receive my newspaper, there is public transportation, the food and theater is excellent. My daughter is even going to receive a Ph.D. at the University of Mesopotamia; why should I give all this up and move to the boonies?"

Ezra led approximately 1,500 people — priests, Levites, singers, gate-keepers, etc. — back to Jerusalem. Oh, and incidentally there were a number of reasons, or shall we say inducements, for people to accompany him on this migration. The people who immigrated would be exempt from paying local and royal taxes. Like the *halutzim* who gave up everything and moved to Palestine, these people took the risk and this time it included benefits.

Ezra arrived in Jerusalem in 458 B.C.E. carrying with him an official authorization empowering him to appoint judges and to judge in accordance with the law of the God of Heaven. His authority also granted him the rite to administer capital punishment. The king also authorized Ezra to receive a special allocation from the royal treasury and to institute the Temple sacrifices to the king and his family. The king bequeathed to Ezra the Temple vessels of silver and gold. This was the pattern of Babylonian kings who endowed temples in sacred cities.

Ezra's main concern was to separate the community of the returnees from those who had not undergone the experience of exile. In his book he refers to himself and those who lived in Babylon as *b'nai hagolah* (people of the exile) and his adversaries as *am ha-aretz* (people of the land). Ezra transformed this phrase into a derogatory expression.

Apparently he summoned the leading Jerusalem families to a meeting and demanded they separate from their alien wives. If you read his book you will note that Ezra is concerned with maintaining the purity of Jewish blood. In order to be considered a Jew, according to Ezra, one needed Jewish blood. He might have been considered the lawgiver, but our tradition also embraced the story of Ruth, the story of a non-Jewish woman, a product of two non-sanctioned biblical marriages, whose descendant was King David.

It is possible that the story of Ruth, which is read perhaps not coincidently on Shavout, the festival commemorating our receiving Divine Law, was written to counter Ezra's xenophobia and to demonstrate that sincere devout people are more important than racial or blood profiling. Malachi, **Malachi** the last of the prophets, is linked to the Ezra period because he expresses a similar attitude toward intermarriage. This helps us date the text and his ministry.

Ezra's effort to separate intermarrieds was not successful. It is possible he was forced to retract his order owing to changes in the international situation or as a result of complaints lodged on behalf of the noble families in Jerusalem.

Also at that time, I saw the Jews had married Ashdodite, Ammonite, and Moabite women; a good number of their children spoke the language of Ashdod and the language of those various peoples, and did not know how to speak Judean. I censured them, cursed them, flogged them, tore out their hair, and adjured them by God, saying, "You shall not give your daughters in marriage to their sons, or take any of their daughters for your sons or yourselves. It was just in such things that King Solomon of Israel sinned! Foreign wives caused even him to sin. How, then, can we acquiesce in your doing this great wrong, breaking faith with our God by marrying foreign women? One of the sons' of Joiada son of the high priest Eliashib was a son-in-law of Sanballat the Horonite; I drove him away from me. Remember to their credit, O my God, how they polluted the priesthood, the covenant of the priests and the Levites. I purged them of every foreign element." (Ezra 13:23)

The rabbis credit Ezra with returning to Jerusalem along with the Torah. He allegedly established the text of the Pentateuch, introducing the Assyrian or the square script that we read today. He is also credited with decreeing that three people should read ten verses from the Torah on the second and fifth days of the week and during the afternoon (Minchah) service on Shabbat. The Talmud considers Ezra to be a second Moses.

The book of Malachi closes the second part of the Bible. If we date this in accordance with how the text reads or around the time of Ezra, we would conclude that the prophetic canon was closed around 420 B.C.E. Actually, this section of the Tanaach was most likely completed one hundred to two hundred years later—that is to say, sometime towards the end of the Persian period or near the beginning of the Greek period.

Toldot

Shabbat HaGadol

Malachi consists of three chapters and yet warrants two haftarot (parshat Toldot and parshat Shabbat HaGadol)! While Haggai anticipates the rebuilding of the shrine and Zechariah is concerned with its rebuilding and its sanctity,

Malachi lived after the Temple's construction had been completed.

The purpose of his book is to challenge the readers to look at some of the pitfalls of everyday life, including what took place once the Temple had been rebuilt. Malachi was distressed with the way Temple worship and practice had devolved. Like so many of us today, and like Solomon of ancient times, the Temple was a symbol that motivated and united a people, but once it had been completed the spirit that created it became corrupt.

Malachi believed that a corrupt clergy and improper personal behaviors damaged the relationship between God and Israel. The results of this damaged relationship resulted in a lack of prosperity. Malachi was concerned that people should sacrifice and tithe honestly. He was also upset with the high rate of intermarriage which existed in Jerusalem society and attempted to reform current priestly behaviors. Interesting that the behaviors of public officials and the attitude toward intermarriage have not left us.

The rabbis in Talmudic times disagree about who Malachi actually was. Some say he was Ezra. Others claim he was **The Great** one of the members of The Great Assembly. It doesn't **Assembly** matter.

> When the last prophets, Haggai, Zechariah, and Malachi died, the Holy Spirit departed from Israel. (Tosephta Sotah 8:2)

The period which began with Joshua (the first of the prophets) and ended with Malachi lasted approximately 800 years. After that, the Talmud speaks of people who hear a *bat kol*, a heavenly voice. The rabbis discouraged this form of revelation.

Some people believe that the scroll that Ezra carried with him from Babylon was composed of five books: Genesis, Exodus, Leviticus, Numbers, and Deuteronomy. It is possible, but what is likely is that from this point onward legitimate prophecy in Israel ceased to exist. Inspiration was no longer received through prophets and was replaced by the gift of Ezra, the written word. From this time onward, our ancestors, priests, scribes, and eventually rabbis sought inspiration through a written text.

The rabbis consider these three prophets and Ezra to be the first members of what came to be called The Great Assembly. Our tradition credits these men with the responsibility of transmitting the tradition that was first given to Moses at Sinai. While our literature continued to highlight wonderworkers and mystics, the development and study of the law replaced them and began to serve as the source of inspiration for future Jewish tradition.

CONCLUSION

If I could extract a few ideas or themes from all of the haftarot, one of them would be the recognition that the Prophets were political activists. It appears that most of them were concerned with either personal, priestly, or national behaviors accompanied by strong words of caution to anyone who was in the process of striking a political bargain. They weren't afraid to take risks and they were aware that the nature of one's message could change depending upon the circumstances of the time.

The rabbis, who extracted selections from the prophetic works and transformed them into haftarot, viewed them through a different lens. They most likely understood the prophetic words as warnings communicated across hundreds of years, and in some instances an equal number of miles, that could advise future and different generations how to potentially avoid repeating the errors of the past.

When I read a haftarah I always ask myself, "Why was this haftarah selected and what were the circumstances when the haftarah allegedly took place?" Having asked those questions I try to understand the nature of the two messages most likely to have been embedded in these texts that I need to learn.

The Prophets and the people who selected the texts to serve as haftarot have, for a variety of reasons, had an impact on the development of Judaism. As I read their words week after week I realize they were people who lived, as do we all, in tumultuous times. The ways they responded to their realities shaped future generations. Some of them attempted to warn our ancestors. Others gave up a more sophisticated life in the major city of the time to become pioneers committed to the rebuilding of our ancient land. It was one of the tasks of the rabbinate to reinterpret the religious traditions of the prophets in order to provide vision, meaning, and guidance to the lives of the people with whom they lived.

It is possible that the messages that can be learned from viewing the texts from both lenses can help us to continuously find new meanings within them that will offer guidance to each generation, no matter what challenges they/we face.

Appendix

....

The Origins and Development of the Haftarah Blessings

The development of the haftarah blessings and their subsequent implementation took place over a time period of minimally one hundred years and possibly as much as three hundred years. One might assume that the implementation of the haftarah readings paralleled the implementation of the Torah readings, but that's not the case. The Torah, as we know it, arrived with Ezra in 480 B.C.E. The second section of the Bible, the Prophets, probably took final form sometime 250–300 years later.

When Ezra initiated the Torah readings they probably didn't include every Shabbat and holiday Torah reading, at least not all at once. What probably occurred was the first Torah readings took place on the biblical festivals, Rosh Hashanah, Yom Kippur, Sukkoth, Passover, and Shavuot. At some point after the readings had been accepted and established, the Torah readings for the four special Shabbatot prior to Passover were added. This was followed by the next phase of implementation, which added the regular readings for Mondays and Thursdays and *Rosh Chodesh*. Finally, perhaps as late as the fourth century, the special Torah readings for Hanukkah and Purim were added.

It is probable that the blessings before and after the Torah were finalized sometime in the 3rd or 4th centuries C.E. By that time, the regular Torah readings had become more or less standardized and the transition from a triennial cycle to an annual cycle had taken place. When the Torah was read on a triennial basis, selected verses from the Prophets, most likely between three and ten verses, were read or chanted after the Torah reading. These selections were called haftarot, from the word *peter*, which means "to end." They were connected to the Torah reading thematically or

73

because a phrase or two had some connection which would link it to the Torah reading.

The blessings before and after the haftarah readings were probably standardized at the same time. They were organized around 300 C.E. by a man who our texts refer to as Rav, the Teacher of the entire Diaspora. Rav was born in Babylonia to a distinguished family and moved to Israel to study with Rabbi Hiyya. He joined the academy of Judah ha-Nasi. He explained the purpose of the mitzvoth in the following manner: *"the mitzvot were only given as a means of refining people."*

....

The Structure of the Haftarah Blessings

The haftarah blessings are composed of one introductory blessing and four blessings which are chanted after the selection from the Prophets has been completed.

The introductory blessing links the validity of the prophets to Moses. They, like he, were chosen.

> Praised are You Adonai our God, who rules the universe, appointed *devoted Prophets*, and upholding their teachings, messages of truth. Praised are you Adonai, who loves the Torah, Moses His servant, Israel His people and *Prophets of truth and righteousness.*

The first of the concluding blessings begins with a testimony of our faith in God.

> Praised are You Adonai our God, who rules the universe, Rock of ages, righteous in all generations, steadfast God whose word is deed, whose decree is fulfillment, whose every teaching is truth, and righteousness. Faithful are You Adonai our God, in all Your promises, of which not one will remain unfulfilled, for You are a faithful and merciful God

74

and Sovereign. Praised are You Adonai, God faithful in all Your promises.

The second blessing raises several interesting questions:

Show compassion for Zion, the fount of our existence, and bring hope soon to the humbled spirit. Praised are You Adonai, who brings joy to Zion.

The first question is why should God show compassion and what has occurred to warrant it? In an earlier form of this blessing the word *rachem* ("show compassion") is not present. Instead the word *nachem*, meaning "comfort us," was employed. Perhaps at a time closer to the Bar Kokbah rebellion one would ask for comfort. After all, one comforts a mourner. On the other hand, one shows compassion for other reasons, perhaps reasons of love.

Another interesting development is the translation of the Hebrew phrase *vlaoovat nefesh*, which translates in Siddur Sim Shalom as *and bring hope soon to the humble spirit*. However, earlier versions of Rabbinical Assembly siddurim and other siddurim translated this phrase to mean *and take vengeance on behalf of the sorrowful (miserable)*.

An earlier version, perhaps the earliest version of the blessings employed the phrase *vlaoogomot nefesh tnakem, save us from affliction of spirit*. This translation reflects a time when our ancestors lived through what they would have considered to be the Holocaust of their time. Their spirits were afflicted. The impact of the destruction of the Temple and the failure of the Bar Kokbah rebellion had a disastrous effect on their lives. Yet some time later, they desired to stop mourning and began to pray for hope as they strove to become more humble and God-fearing individuals. Perhaps in the aftermath, the rabbis of the time recognized that the world was changing and new approaches to providing meaning to ensuring the future of Jewish life were required.

A huge theological and emotional gap exists between the language of the oldest blessing, which pleads for God to save his people from an affliction of spirit, and a later translation that pleads for vengeance and eventually evolves into a desire for us to become humble people.

The third blessing begins with the word *Samchenu* and means "make us happy."

> Bring us joy, Adonai, our God, through Your prophet Elijah and the kingdom of the House of David Your anointed. May Elijah come soon, to gladden our hearts. May no outsider usurp David's throne, and may no other inherit his glory. For by Your holy name have You promised that his light shall never be extinguished. Praised are You Adonai, Shield of David.

The earliest version of this text states *m'nachemenu*, meaning "console us" instead of *bring us joy*. This is a fascinating blessing. It began as a prayer for consolation and was replaced by one that requests joy. Could it be that the period of metaphoric mourning, whatever it was, had passed and a new outlook on life was called for?

This blessing also refers to the Messiah and hopes that he might come speedily in our days.

In the aftermath of the Second Temple's destruction in 70 C.E. and after the failure of the Bar Kokbah revolt where Akiba had declared him to be the Messiah, using words like the "Messiah" could have had serious implications.

Remember: In the Passover story there is the story of five rabbis on the Seder night in Bene-barak. At one point one of the students calls out and reminds them that it was time to recite the morning *Shema*.

This insert wasn't about a prayer. If one studies the entire traditional Haggadah before it was translated by Maxwell House, it becomes obvious that much of our haggadot were written in code. Legend has it that the five rabbis in the upper chambers of Bene-Brak were plotting what came to be called the Bar Kokhbah rebellion. One of these five rabbis was Rabbi Akiba, the man who proclaimed Bar Kokbah to be the messiah!

The results of the revolt were tragic and Akiba was incarcerated and eventually tortured to death. We read about his death in the martyrology on Yom Kippur.

In order for references to the Messiah to become part of our liturgy, they needed to be understood and taught in an entirely different manner from the way Akiba understood it in 135 C.E.

The Talmud shares what rabbis living after the Bar Kokbah rebellion thought about the messiah. (Sources: Talmud Sanhedrin chapter 10, page 97a.)

> It has been taught: R. Nehorai said: In the generation when Messiah comes, young men will insult the old, and old men will stand before the young to give them honor. Daughters will rise up against their mothers, and daughters-in-law against their mothers-in-law.

> It has been taught. R. Nehemiah said: in the generation of Messiah's coming impudence will increase, esteem be perverted, the vine yield its fruit, yet shall wine be dear. And the Kingdom will be converted to heresy with none to rebuke them. The son of David will not come until the whole world is converted to the belief of the heretics.

> Another interpretation until scholars are few. Until the redemption is despaired.

> R. Hama b. Hanina said: The son of David will not come until even the pettiest kingdom ceases to have power over Israel.

> The son of David will not come until there are no conceited men in Israel.

> The son of David will not come until all judges and officers are gone from Israel.

Rabi Johanan (250–290 C.E.) also said, the son of David will come only in a generation that is either altogether righteous or altogether wicked.

R. Joshua b. Levi (first half of the 3rd century, Israel) said, if they are worthy.

The rabbis living 75–250 years later certainly weren't revolutionaries like Akiba. If anything, they were pacifists! Their concept of the Messiah was unclear and certainly not revolutionary. Unlike Akiba, who believed one could bring the Messiah to earth, the rabbis living two to three hundred years later believed the Messiah was a concept or perhaps a symbol of universal redemption. According to this blessing the Messiah would only arrive after he was announced by Elijah. The blessing also links redemption to the house of David.

Why did these changes occur?

Perhaps a sufficient period of time had passed and the psychological horror of the Temple's destruction and the trauma of the Bar Kokbah rebellion had diminished. Living under Roman rule in the third century had its benefits, and our ancestors began to see joy and gladness in the world. The desire which emerged for appreciating life and living as an ethical person was supplemented by a new theology that preached a life of Torah would lead to becoming an ethical person.

In order to preserve the memory of the Temple and the kingdom of David, a new interpretation of Jewish living emerged that was not revolutionary and sought to keep a people separate, viable, and committed to living a religious life. The rabbis who shaped the haftarah blessings and the haftarot themselves had studied the history of the prophetic period and through the haftarot attempted to teach what they believed to be lessons that would ensure Jewish continuity.

The Torah/Haftarah Relationship

What criteria and selection process did the rabbis employ that caused them to select one prophetic portion as a haftarah over another?

That is the question!

The answer is complicated and a number of items need to be considered in order to even make an educated guess. Educated guesses or conjectural assumptions are appropriate words to use in this matter because very little actual information is available.

We do know that at least three traditions of reading from the prophets were in existence prior to the current annual Babylonian tradition becoming dominant. Scholars conjecture that an annual Torah reading took place in Palestine and in Babylon. Some scholars postulate that a triennial Torah reading also was in existence at the same time in Galilee. The triennial and annual cycles could have originated in Palestine but it has yet to be proved.

Several different traditions of triennial haftarot exist. Some of them consisted of 154 selections, others as many as 178. Most people assume that the triennial Torah cycle completed the reading of the Torah in three years; yet some traditions claim that it took three and one half years. Unlike the Babylonian and current tradition where the Torah reading for the next week is read on Shabbat Minha and Monday and Thursday mornings, the triennial reading was consecutive—that is to say, that prior to the Temple's destruction a person would read a certain number of lines; let's say 2, 3, or 4. The person who followed would read what he wished, perhaps 3, 5, or 10 verses, and the third person would read as many as he wished to read. Wherever the three concluded would serve as the starting point for the following week. This resulted in a lack of order and might have been one of the reasons that led to the adoption of the annual Babylonian system which we follow today.

The Palestinian triennial calendar was also more fixed to the reading cycle. Simhat Torah, for example, would take place at the conclusion of the reading of the book of Deuteronomy. This is unlike our current system when it is celebrated at the end of Sukkoth.

The connecting of prophetic passages to Torah portions didn't happen all at once. It was more likely a result of a centuries-long process. The first haftarot were probably linked to Torah portions during major festivals. It is possible that this began to occur during the first or second centuries B.C.E. This was probably followed by special Sabbaths and at some point centuries later, the remaining Torah portions acquired prophetic partners. The haftarot excerpted from Jeremiah and Isaiah which correspond to the three weeks prior to the 9th of Av, and the seven weeks which follow, most likely were joined in the 2nd or 3rd centuries C.E. We can assume this to be the case because the tradition existed in both Babylon and Palestine. If one compares the two traditions one finds that forty-two of what are generally assumed to be fifty-eight Babylonian haftarot exist in both cycles.

During the first three centuries of the new millennium, a great deal of communication occurred between Palestine and Babylon. Great academies of learning existed in Yavneh, Caesarea, and Tiberius in Palestine and Sura and Pumbedita in Babylon. Its scholars journeyed back and forth and studied and taught at these academies. But by the beginning of the fourth century, contact between Palestine and Babylon practically ceased and didn't reoccur until the end of the Arab expansion. Anecdotally, what is today referred to as the Sephardic haftarot developed out of the Babylonian tradition.

A number of scholars, most currently Michael Fishbane, are of the belief that the haftarot, in many instances where the connection seems tenuous at best, were connected to the Torah portions as a result of the poetic cultural worldview of the leading scholars of the time. In other words there are places where the connection was obvious and others where those seeking to create a connection between the two were forced to rely on their creative and poetic abilities. That makes sense to me.

The Talmud informs us that certain prophetic selections should correspond to specific Torah portions and certain selections, like the first chapter of the book of Ezekiel, were forbidden to serve as haftarot. Our custom today does not conform to their pronouncements, which reinforces the idea that the haftarot were selected over a period of time. The Talmud records that in the mid–4th century a man referred to as "Rav" joined a specific haftarah to parshat *Tzav*. This statement, at so late a date, could be indicative of one of two things. It could reflect that at the time all of the haftarot were connected to a Torah portion or it could reflect an isolated instance in a developing process.

It is interesting to note that in the Talmudic period special occasions warranted special haftarot. Private celebrations like a forthcoming wedding or the death of a scholar sometimes interrupted the routine Prophetic selections and different passages were substituted. For example, it was the custom on the Sabbaths preceding a wedding to read a selection from Isaiah 61:10 to harmonize the text with the wedding celebration.

> I will greatly rejoice in the Lord,
> My whole being exults in my God.
> For He has clothed me with garments of triumph,
> Wrapped me in a robe of victory,
> Like a bridegroom adorned with a turban, like a
> bride bedecked with her finery.
> (Isaiah 61:10)

All of the haftarot were joined to a Torah portion by the 7th century, in what is referred to as the "Gaonic Period."

The creation and inclusion of haftarot reflect the attempt of those living in the aftermath of the Temple's destruction, the Bar Kokbah revolt and the rise of Christianity, to imbue commitment and meaning to a persecuted or at least a dispersed minority. Through what they perceived to be the wisdom, poetry, and inspiration of those who lived in an earlier time, the rabbis attempted to use these texts which were considered to be imbued with "holiness" to educate, involve, and guide our people.

The process of selecting texts from a later period and employing them as educational tools isn't that different from what we attempt to do today. We, like they, attempt to convey a strong connection with the Jewish past based upon our people's successes, failures, and triumphs. We, like they, reach across centuries and attempt to interpret our past even though our sensibilities might have changed in order to hopefully develop stronger connections to Jewish life and Jewish living.

Years ago, I thought it would be more meaningful if new prophetic passages that reflected our modern sensibilities and were more in harmony with today's thinking replaced the existing haftarot, and that this would result in haftarot becoming more widely accepted and studied. I was naïve.

Bibliography

1. Baron, Salo Wittmayer. *A Social and Religious History of the Jews.* Columbia University Press, New York, 1969.

2. Ben Sasson, H. H. *A History of the Jewish People.* Harvard University Press, Cambridge, MA, 1976.

3. Berlin, Adele & Brettler, Mark. *The Jewish Study Bible.* Oxford University Press, New York, 2004.

4. Fishbane, Michael. *The JPS Bible Commentary Haftarot.* Jewish Publication Society, Philadelphia, 2002.

5. Grabbe, Lester I. *Ezra-Nehemia.* Routlege Press, NY, 1998.

6. Heschel, A. J. *The Prophets.* The Jewish Publication Society of America, New York, 1963.

7. Leiman, Sid Z. *The Canonization of Hebrew Scripture.* The Connecticut Academy of the Arts and Sciences, New Haven, CT, 1976.

8. Mann, Jacob. *The Bible as Read and Preached in the Old Synagogue.* Union of American Hebrew Congregations, Cincinnati, Ohio, 1940.

9. Mann, Jacob. *The Bible as Read and Preached in the Old Synagogue,* V. 1. Prolegomenon Ben Zion Wacholder, KTAV Publishing, New York, 1971.

10. Nurmela, Risto. *The Levites: Their Emergence as a Second Class Priesthood.* Scholars Press, Atlanta, Georgia, 1998.

11. Polzin, Robert. *Samuel and the Deuteronomist.* Indiana University Press, 1980.

12. Stern, Sascha. *Calendar and Community: A History of the Jewish Calendar, 2nd Century to 10th Century C.E.* Oxford University Press, 2001.

CPSIA information can be obtained at www.ICGtesting.com
Printed in the USA
BVOW071051140513

320675BV00001B/1/P